Instructor's Manual to Accompany

<u>Outlooks and Insights</u>

Fourth Edition

Editors

Paul Eschholz
Alfred Rosa

Prepared by

Chris Bellitto
Karen Bellitto

St. Martin's Press
New York

Manufactured in the United States of America.

98765
fedcba

For information, write:
St. Martin's Press, Inc.
175 Fifth Avenue
New York, NY 10010

ISBN: 0-312-10111-2

Preface

The purpose of this instructor's manual is to familiarize you with the main features of <u>Outlooks and Insights</u>, Fourth Edition, and to share with you the concerns we had in mind as we composed the questions following each selection. Our intent is to save you time and not, of course, to try to dictate answers or classroom strategy. We assume that occasionally you will disagree with an interpretation or emphasis of ours, and undoubtedly you will find new ways to use the materials in <u>Outlooks and Insights</u>. We trust, however, that the suggestions here will be useful at least as starting points.

We draw your attention to the opening section of this manual, "Teaching from <u>Outlooks and Insights</u>." We have devised some features that we believe make <u>Outlooks and Insights</u>, Fourth Edition, unusually productive and helpful among currently available composition readers, and in this opening section we explain what they are, where they may be found, and how we use them in our classes.

We are very much interested in hearing from anyone who has suggestions for improving either <u>Outlooks and Insights</u> or this instructor's manual. Please write to us at the Department of English, 315 Old Mill, University of Vermont, Burlington, Vermont 05405.

Paul Eschholz
Alfred Rosa

Contents

Teaching from *Outlooks and Insights*

    Outlooks and Insights is a thematic reader designed for use in college writing courses. In this new edition of the book, we have tried to bring you an anthology of the very best essays, short stories, and poems to use with your writing students. The 76 selections in the fourth edition--53 essays, 4 speeches, 10 stories, 1 excerpt from a novel, and 8 poems--are all interesting and challenging, yet well within the reach of the average freshman. Thirty-five of these selections are new to this edition. They represent a careful mix of well-known, respected pieces and fresh new selections. All were chosen to stimulate class discussion and to encourage students to write academically sound argumentative essays.

    The book is organized in eight thematic sections that take the student from personal experiences and relationships to broader concerns, such as education, work, language, society, and politics. Within most of the thematic sections are focused subsections that highlight important contemporary issues that concern today's students. Of special note to this edition are two new thematic units. In "Cultural Encounters," five writers with different racial and ethnic backgrounds explore what happens when cultures collide. In "Contemporary Issues," eight writers examine such topics as illiteracy, violence, animal experimentation, global warming, extinction and endangered species, and euthanasia. We trust that you will find these new sections as provocative and engaging as our students have. Here, briefly, is a listing of the topics covered in each thematic section:

1. Private Lives
   Topics: A Sense of Self
                 Turning Points
2. Family and Friends
   Topics: Family Ties
                 The Troubled American Family
                 What Are Friends?
3. Men and Women
   Topics: Gender Roles
                 Men and Women in the Workplace
4. Campus Life
   Topics: Teaching and Learning
                 Campus Issues of the 1990s

5. Language in America
   Topics: Language, Prejudice, and Sexism
                 Language and Persuasion

6. Cultural Encounters

7.   Contemporary Issues

8.   The Individual and Society: Some Classic Statements

The readings within these topical subsections expose students to a variety
of ways of thinking and writing about the same issue and thereby encourage
discussion and debate. Thus students broaden their outlooks on the subject
while at the same time gaining new insights about the specific issue.

Using "On Reading and Writing"

"On Reading and Writing," the introduction to Outlooks and Insights, is
designed to offer students well-grounded, sympathetic, and practical advice
on how to become more active and accurate readers and how to turn what
they read to effective use in their writing. These reasons alone would be
sufficient to make "On Reading and Writing" one of the first assignments in
your course. We think that it is an excellent way to begin your course for
other reasons as well. You are all too well aware of the varying backgrounds, experiences, abilities, and expectations of the students who enter
your course, and assigning "On Reading and Writing" early on is one way of
putting all of your students on an equal footing.
    This introductory essay provides students with an approach to reading
essays, short stories, and poems--an approach that in effect structures the
reading process for them. The first three pages of "On Reading and Writing"
provide basic orientation. They urge students to read not passively but
actively and critically; explain what a freshman anthology is and how it can
be used; and while acknowledging that different people respond differently
to what they read, argue that any work (at least among those they will find
in Outlooks and Insights) has a core meaning on which different people can
agree, and it is that core meaning they should seek to discover as they read.
    The following five pages comprise a brief but detailed course of
instruction in critical reading. In "Getting the Most Out of What You Read,"
we offer specific guidance in comprehension, ranging from the most basic
requirements, such as looking up unfamiliar words in a dictionary, to subtler
ones, such as looking for implications and unstated assumptions. "Some
Tips and Techniques for Reading an Essay" urges at least two readings of
the text, explains how to make annotations, and provides a series of
questions that students may use to test their understanding of whatever
they are reading.
    By reading and discussing "On Reading and Writing" students will
recognize the value of full comprehension as well as the need to analyze and
evaluate what they read. In addition, they will learn how to use the ancillary
materials that accompany each selection in Outlooks and Insights and how
these materials can help them to develop their capabilities as readers as well
as writers. Finally, the introduction, particularly in "Reading George Orwell's
'A Hanging': A Case Study," helps to establish certain realistic expectations

among students with regard to some of the writing they will be doing in your course.

The next to last part of "On Reading and Writing," "Some Notes on Fiction and Poetry," is the briefest possible summary of some basic elements of each genre. It is no comprehensive introduction to literature but rather a sketch of a few distinctive features of stories and poems, designed to give students some points to focus on in case you assign them to write analytical papers on literary works.

New to our introduction "On Reading and Writing" is a section called "Writing a Documented Paper." Here we offer advice on notetaking, integrating source materials into an essay, in-text citation of sources, and compiling a list of works cited. Both MLA and APA styles are discussed. This section concludes with a documented student essay analyzing John Updike's short story "A Sense of Shelter" (p. 64).

Three features that we have found especially useful to emphasize in our classroom discussions of "On Reading and Writing" are the set of questions that appears on page 6 and the case study of Orwell's "A Hanging." The questions are designed to help students focus their attention on the key elements in what they read and should aid them in achieving a thorough understanding of each selection. These questions are offered as a concise set of all-purpose questions for students and you should feel free to elaborate on them or to add to them. We have found these questions so useful in our classes that we reprint them here for your convenience:

1. Do I like the essay or not? What, for me, are the most interesting parts of it? What parts do I find least interesting or hardest to understand?

2. What is the essay's main idea? What are the chief supporting ideas, and how do they relate to the main idea?

3. What is the author's attitude toward the essay's subject? What is the author's purpose? What readers was the author apparently writing for, and what is his or her attitude toward them? How am I part of the intended audience--if I am?

4. How is the essay structured? How does its organization relate to its main idea and to the author's purpose?

5. Can I follow the essay's line of reasoning? Is its logic valid, however complex, or are there mistakes and fallacies? If the reasoning is flawed, how much damage does this do to the essay's effect?

6. Does the author supply enough information to support the essay's ideas, and enough details to make its descriptions precise? Is all of the information relevant and, as far as I know, accurate? Are all of the details convincing? What does the author leave out, and how do these omissions affect my response to the essay?

7. What are the essay's basic, underlying assumptions? Which are stated and which are left unspoken? Are they acceptable, or do I challenge them? If I do, and I am right, how does this affect the essay's main idea?

8. Do all the elements of the essay relate, directly or indirectly, to its main idea? Can I explain how they relate? If any do not, what other purposes do they serve, if any?

9. Where do I place this essay in the context of my other reading? In the context of my life and thought? What further thoughts, and further reading, does it incite me to? Would I recommend it to anyone else to read? To whom, and why?

All of these questions work best when students try to answer them as fully as they can, remembering and considering many details from the selection to support their answers. Most of the questions are variations on these three basic queries: "What's going on here?" and "why?" and "How do I feel about it?"

We use "Reading George Orwell's 'A Hanging': A Case Study" in its entirety and encourage you to do likewise. First we have students read "A Hanging" in preparation for class discussion. Students should be encouraged to take notes both during and after their reading. You can then use the reading questions reprinted above to shape and direct the ensuing class discussion. Finally, students have told us that they have profited from a discussion of the three student essays (p. 14). These three essays, each different from the others and from Orwell's, illustrate a few of the many different ways people can respond to their reading and use their responses in their writing. We like to analyze each of the essays with students in class in terms of both content and form; this leads the students to a common understanding of what is expected of them in the course. In order to give you some idea of the kinds of concerns covered in our discussion of each essay, we reprint below "The Disgrace of Man," the first student essay, along with our teaching notes.

The Disgrace of Man	title clearly states writer's theme
George Orwell's "A Hanging" graphically depicts the execution of a prisoner in a way that expresses a universal tragedy. He artfully employs metaphor, personification, and dialogue to indicate man's inhumanity toward other men, and to prompt the reader's sympathy and self-examination.	opening paragraph introduces theme and presents thesis, and establishes a three-part organizational sequence
Orwell uses simile and metaphor to show that the	Part I: Orwell's use of metaphor

prisoner is treated more like an animal than like a human being. The cells of the condemned men, "a row of sheds . . . quite bare within," are "like small animal cages." The wardens grip the prisoner "like men handling a fish." Though they refer to the prisoner as "the man" or "our friend," the other characters view him as less than human. Even his cry resounds like the "tolling of a bell" rather than a human "prayer or cry for help," and after he is dead the superintendent pokes at the body with a stick. These details direct the reader's attention to the lack of human concern for the condemned prisoner.

    In contrast, Orwell emphasizes the "wrongness of cutting a life short" by representing the parts of the prisoner's body as taking on human behavior. He describes the "lock of hair "dancing" on the man's scalp, his feet "printing themselves" on the gravel, all his organs "toiling away" like a team of laborers at some collective project. In personifying these bodily features, Orwell forces the reader to see the prisoner's vitality, his humanity. The reader, in turn, associates each bodily part with himself; he becomes highly aware of the frailty of life. As the author focuses on how easily these actions can be stopped, in any human being, "with a sudden snap," the reader feels the "wrongness" of the hanging as if his own life were threatened.

examples

effect upon reader

Part II: Orwell's use of personification

examples

effect upon reader

In addition to creating this sense of unmistakable life, Orwell uses the dog as a standard for evaluating the characters' appreciation of human life. The dog loves people-- he is "wild with glee to find so many human beings together"--and the person he loves the most is the prisoner, who has been treated as less than human by the jail attendants. When the prisoner starts to pray, the other people are silent, but the dog answers "with a whine." Even after the hanging, the dog runs directly to the gallows to see the prisoner again. The reader is forced to reflect on his own reaction: Which is more shocking, the dog's actions or the observers' cold response?

examples

Finally, Orwell refers to the characters' nationalities to stress that this insensitivity extends to all nationalities and races. The hanging takes place in Burma, in a jail run by a European army doctor and a native of southern India. The warders are also Indians, and the hangman is actually a fellow prisoner. The author calls attention to each of these participants and implies that each one of them might have halted the brutal proceedings. He was there too and could have intervened when he suddenly realized that killing the prisoner would be wrong. Yet the "formality of the hanging" goes on.

examples

As he reflects on the meaning of suddenly destroying human life, Orwell emphasizes the similarities among all men, regardless of nationality. Before the hanging, they are "seeing, hearing, feeling, understanding the same world," and afterward there would be "one mind less, one world less." Such feelings do not affect the other characters, who think of the hanging not as a killing but as a job to be done, a job made unpleasant by those reminders (the incident of the dog, the prisoner's praying) that they are dealing with a human being. Orwell uses dialogue to show how selfish and callous the observers are. Though they have different accents--the superintendent's "for God's sake hurry up," the Dravidian's "It was all finished"--they think and feel the same. Their words, such as "He's all right," show that they are more concerned about their own lives than the one they are destroying.

Part III: Orwell's use of dialogue

examples

Although George Orwell sets his story in Burma, his point is universal; although he deals with capital punishment, he implies other questions of life and death. We are all faced with issues such as capital punishment, abortion, and euthanasia, and sometimes we find ourselves directly involved, as Orwell did. "A Hanging" urges us to examine ourselves and to take very seriously the value of a human life.

conclusion

restatement of thesis

After going over this essay with your students, you may want to assign the other two essays, "For Capital Punishment" and "Killing for Fun," for them to analyze independently.

Using the Selections in <u>Outlooks and Insights</u>

Each section of <u>Outlooks and Insights</u> begins with some provocative epigraphs that touch upon the topics of each subsection in the unit. They establish the range of the theme and chart out the territory for students before they begin reading the individual selections.

The epigraphs can be used as the basis for discussion and writing assignments. Most of our epigraphs amount to pithy but unsupported thesis statements and can be developed or rebutted.

We introduce each selection with a biographical headnote that sets the piece in the context of the author's work and supplies information about the author's original audience and purpose. Because of this relationship between a headnote and the selection it introduces, students would do well to read the headnote before proceeding to read the selection itself.

The questions and writing topics supplied for each selection further develop and exploit the advice and instruction given in "On Reading and Writing." The study questions about each essay, story, and poem, like the general questions in the introduction, help students to test and increase their understanding of what they have read, and may also help them gather material for analytical papers. Some questions ask for the selection's thesis, or main idea; others, about specific details within the selection; and still others, about aspects of the selection's organization and style. The writing topics suggest a few ways that students may use a reading in their writing or to start them on their own lines of thought.

Students should also be encouraged to read the selections for an understanding and an appreciation of form and technique. And to that end some study questions address such rhetorical considerations as organization, tone, audience, and style in a nontechnical manner. If you want to spend class time working on a particular rhetorical mode (argumentation, for example), you will find our rhetorical table of contents particularly helpful in planning your assignments. (The rhetorical table of contents appears on pages xv-xxi of <u>Outlooks and Insights</u>.) Finally, don't forget to point out to your students the glossary of useful literary and rhetorical terms beginning on page 617 of the text, so that they can consult it when needed.

Most of this manual is devoted to our notes on the questions--the answers we would give, the way we would handle discussion of the question in class, the points we would look for in a student essay growing out of one of the writing topics. Perhaps you will disagree with our interpretations on occasion, or sometimes find your own writing assignments more fitting. Nonetheless we offer our answers, if only to reveal what we had in mind with our questions, and hope you may find them useful.

Using Outlooks and Insights for Writing

As you can see, Outlooks and Insights offers a variety of materials and ways for students to use them in your writing course. We suggest that you have your students:

--Write about one or more of the section epigraphs.

--Write analytical essays about the readings. The general questions in "On Reading and Writing" and the specific questions that follow each selection, help them get started.

--Write essays in response to the writing topics that follow each reading. These are designed to elicit results ranging from autobiographical essays and arguments to research papers.

Of course, it always makes good pedagogical sense not to give the same type of writing assignment too often to the same class, but to vary their assignments to help develop versatility. And don't overlook one of the richest resources for students seeking to discover ideas for their writing: the classroom discussions you conduct on each reading.

A Sense of Self

Shame

Dick Gregory

Questions for Study and Discussion (p. 49)

    1. Shame for Gregory is a lack of self-respect and the respect of others, because of his family's poverty and lack of a father, and his feelings of shame are brought on by his teacher's revealing those conditions. In paragraph 28 he says, "Now there was shame everywhere. It seemed like the whole world had been inside that classroom, everyone had heard what the teacher had said, everyone had turned around and felt sorry for me."

    2. Gregory's opinion of his teacher's attitude is detailed in paragraphs 5 and 6. That attitude is also expressed by her revealing to the class Gregory's lack of a father (and her facial expression while so doing-- paragraphs 20 and 22) and by her reference to "you and your kind" (20). Her choosing him to wash blackboards for her (25) made him think she liked him, but in the context of the story she may have had another reason; most children detest being kept after school.

    3. Throughout the story, money is a symbol of prestige that can "buy" attention, respect, and even "a Daddy" (7). Gregory drops money on Helene's stoop, and he can forget her only after he is "making money" (3). Gregory's effort to contribute to the Community Chest is a direct public bid for respect. In the final incident of the story, Gregory meets a tramp who has self-respect and is not ashamed of his poverty.

    4. A number of details are mentioned in passing within the essay: the lack of water and central heat in the apartment (1), the lack of adequate meals and proper food (5, 25), that Gregory had few clothes and no shoes and shared his bed with five other people (5), and that he shined shoes and sold newspapers to make extra money (29). We can infer that the apartment must have been dingy, crowded, hot in summer and cold in winter, and that Gregory's mother was harassed and overworked and gave him little attention or emotional support.

    5. The repetition of the words shame and money keep the story's theme constantly in the foreground. These are emotionally evocative words, and many students will surely mention the impact of those words on their feelings. Other repetitions include pregnant (5) to indicate Gregory's preoccupation with poverty; Helene and Helene Tucker (especially in

paragraph 3), who is "a symbol of everything you want" (2); and <u>Daddy</u>, so different in connotation from <u>father</u>.

<u>Writing Topics (p. 49)</u>

1. The purpose of this assignment is to elicit narratives of significant personal experiences, and not necessarily humiliating ones such as Gregory's. "Shame" can nonetheless serve as a good model because it recaptures in precise detail the situation that elicited Gregory's feelings of shame. Similarly, students should be encouraged to show what happened, using as much detail as possible before going on to tell what the incident meant to them then and now.

2. This assignment is like topic 1 above, but more general in scope. A class discussion of some institutions and organizations (for example, school and college, church, the Scouts, athletic teams) may suggest possible topics. Such institutions may reward individualism or squelch it, support self-esteem or damage it, and so on. The resulting compositions may include narrative but should also analyze cause and effect.

3. Students readily engage in a discussion of their reactions to peoples' dress, behavior, weight, height, hair style, and speech. Oftentimes they are not aware how strongly, in either a positive or negative sense, these factors affect interpersonal relationships. After ten or fifteen minutes of discussion, ask students to do a free-write about an experience they have had in which appearance was a good indicator of self-image.

Shooting an Elephant

George Orwell

<u>Questions for Study and Discussion (p. 56)</u>

1. The setting of the story is Lower Burma, which, at the time of the incident, was part of Britain's colonial empire. Since Orwell narrates the story in order to illustrate the dynamics of imperialism, the setting is crucial to the story. Orwell writes in his essay about "the hollowness, the futility of the white man's dominion in the East" (7) and observes that "when the white man turns tyrant it is his own freedom he destroys" (7).

2. At the conclusion of the essay Orwell explains that he shot the elephant "solely to avoid looking a fool." Earlier in paragraph 7 he notes that he did it because the natives expected him to do so. Some students may wonder, however, whether Orwell was not also afraid of being trampled by the elephant. He says this is not so (9), but his vivid description of the dead coolie (4) and his awareness of the physical danger to himself (9) may lead

students to read between the lines. We would say only that the text does not directly support such an interpretation.

3. In paragraph 7 Orwell states the point of the story, which is "the hollowness, the futility of the white man's dominion in the East. . . . When the white man turns tyrant it is his own freedom that he destroys. . . . In every crisis he has got to do what the 'natives' expect o him." See also paragraphs 2 to 3, 7, 9, and 14.

4. At this point you may wish to select various passages to examine the remarkable detail that Orwell conveys. The description of the elephant in particular is a masterpiece of diction. Note for instance the elephant's "preoccupied grandmotherly air" (8) and the precise verbs Orwell chooses. The slowness of the animal's death is captured through sentence rhythm and structure, for example, in the numerous compound-complex sentences in the section, which seem to imitate the elephant's prolonged agony.

5. In the final paragraph Orwell presents a series of rationalizations for the shooting, then sweeps them all away with his final sentence. His refusal to make excuses for himself--even to plead that he acted in self-defense--is typical of Orwell's merciless honesty.

Writing Topics (p. 56)

1. As Orwell's essay demonstrates, a crowd or even a compact group takes on a larger but less rational presence than an individual. The followers are apt to react in a more primitive, unreflective manner than they would as leaders.

2. The assignment requires students to present a conflict dynamically and to reflect on and analyze the significance of their actions. It may be useful for students to organize their essay into three parts: a brief beginning in which they describe their convictions; a middle portion in which they present the conflict with as much vividness as possible, analyzing the reasons for and constraints upon their actions; and finally a discussion of whatever conclusions they have drawn from the incident.

3. It is useful to have a general discussion of imperialism before the students research their topic, as the word has been used loosely and propagandistically in recent years. It may also be useful to consider the imperialists' self-justifications. Some such arguments are that they were "civilizing" the "heathen," that they were protecting an internal minority from hostile internal forces, that they were forwarding the country's economic development, or that they were protecting the country from other, more pernicious imperial powers. In their research, students may want to focus on a particular example of imperialism.

How It Feels to Be Colored Me

Zora Neale Hurston

<u>Questions for Study and Discussion (p. 60)</u>

1. Until Hurston's thirteenth birthday, Southern and Northern whites were different from her in their habits, not in their color. However, the day she left Eatonville she entered a world in which she was distinguished by her color from the whites around her. Her "colored" self is a member of a race, one among many, "thrown against a sharp white background," but not tragically so. "Slavery is the price I paid for civilization, and the choice was not with me." (7) Her "no race" self rejoices in Zora, the self who is "merely a fragment of the Great Soul that surges within the boundaries." (15)

2. Hurston holds no malice, seeks no revenge; more, she pities the oppressors of her race, who can never experience the exhilaration of the struggle for civilization and recognition that her forebears had. Her attitude suggests a vital, joyful, generous woman who takes pride in her humanity without the necessity of belittling others. Throughout the essay she expresses her pleasure in life with her use of phrases such as: "a born first-nighter," (3); "I wanted to do them [dance, sing, and recite] so much that I needed bribing to stop," (4); "When I set my hat at a certain angle and saunter down Seventh Avenue, Harlem City . . ." (14).

3. The "brown specter" and the "dark ghost" are the threat to whites of the progress of African-Americans in our culture. Any knowledge of groups such as the Ku Klux Klan should convince readers that there are groups of whites who fear and work against the advancement of people of color.

4. In her nightclub fantasy, Hurston dresses herself in the traditional garb of the African native, inviting the reader to feel the excitement and color of her frenzy. By contrast, the white companion is colorless for his lack of rhythm and appreciation of the music. This distinction may be fair in the instance she recounts only because Hurston exhibits an enthusiasm that few people of any color can lay claim to. However, some students may argue that in all races there are people capable of enthusiasm and wild abandon.

5. Hurston compares people to a bag of assorted items, junk mixed with treasure. While the exterior is easy to identify as one color or another, the contents defy differentiation. Her analogy works well in making the simple point that all people are the same inside since they have the same maker. She reveals again, her generous, all embracing view of humanity, although in reality her vision does not play itself out.

4

1. Students may find it easier to approach this topic if they first consider what major differences or similarities exist between Gregory's essay and Hurston's essay. Before students begin this assignment it may be helpful to review elements of comparison and contrast.

2. As a prewriting discussion you may wish to have the students come up with a list of people who, although oppressed seem to maintain a positive self-image. If the list reflects people discriminated against for different reasons (for example, race, sex, or religion), ask the students whether these people have common characteristics. You may also ask students to speculate on what influenced these positive images.

3. As students develop their essays on this topic, they should consider whether they can identify specific social circumstances that might have led to a more positive self-image. They may be able to compare the experiences of another person who has the same trait and how their self-image has fared. You may also have them consider how much location has been a factor in their handling of this concern and how others have treated them.

I'm Nobody! Who Are You?

Emily Dickinson

Questions for Study and Discussion (p. 62)

1. It sounds as if the speaker wants to remain anonymous and be a "nobody." If the reader is another "nobody," then the speaker and reader can enjoy a special closeness, apart from the public world of "somebodies." "They" are the "somebodies" determined that everyone should live as publicly and superficially as they do.

2. Since she was such a recluse, it would appear that Dickinson did not want to become "somebody" because that would mean becoming entangled in the world of publicity and self-advertisement--a world she compares to a "bog."

3. Two answers may be plausible. First, children enjoy thinking of themselves as secret observers of the adult world, so the poem would appeal to them. On the other hand, children are apt to try to fit in and play-act in order to conform to the crowd. This poem tells them that they do not have to: They are uniquely special.

4. Dickinson comes across in the first stanza as playful, childlike, perhaps a bit flirtatious. In the second stanza, she quickly becomes surprisingly sarcastic and patronizing toward the public world of "somebodies."

Writing Topics (p. 63)

1. Students may wish to compare their life to that of someone famous (for example, Michael Jackson, President Clinton, a sports figure). They may wish to write about how they think they would react to notoriety and constant attention. Ask them to put themselves in the spotlight and discuss both the pros and cons of constant media attention.

2. Answers will vary according to the student. One common theme that can be brought out in discussion or sharing of essays is how the appearance or anticipation of an important event or accomplishment matched the reality of the achievement itself.

3. Students may find that the reason Dickinson was not published during her lifetime was because she was a woman in a man's world, writing poems unconventional in form and subject matter. They might also consider her rather eccentric personality and how it is captured in her poetry.

A Sense of Shelter

John Updike

Questions for Study and Discussion (p. 73)

1. In paragraph 10 William imagines the successful course of his life: "high school merging into college, college into graduate school, graduate school into teaching at a college--section man, assistant, associate, <u>full</u> professor, professor of a dozen languages and a thousand books, a man brilliant in his forties, wise in his fifties, renowned in his sixties, revered in his seventies, and then retired." For other indications of William's view of himself, see paragraph 2. From the numerous details Updike supplies, the reader can build a detailed picture of William: a shy, introverted boy who nevertheless has a high opinion of himself, who knows how to obtain his elders' approval but not how to relate to his contemporaries, and who is essentially detached and incapable of emotional commitment.

2. In many ways Mary Landis is William's opposite: popular, self-confident, athletic, and sexually experienced. Unlike William, she had always been "at the center of whatever gang was the best one" (9). We see her almost entirely through William's eyes, and it is clear that he sees her as a sex object--he is intensely aware of her appearance, of her "thin, athletic legs" and "pronged chest" (4), and when she asks him what he knows about her he tries to move their relationship onto a sexual plan by replying "that you're not a virgin" (51). His saying he loves her and wants to marry her is at least partly a sexual ploy; in the 1950s it was an almost obligatory gesture. But though she knows others see her as a sex object (4), she does

not like it (43, 51), and her experience of love and life enables her to see through him (54).

3. Throughout the conversation Updike keeps us apprised of William's feelings, from his initial amazement that Mary seems glad to see him to his surprise at her attitude toward his boldness, his embarrassment, and his final humiliation. Since William is so self-absorbed and knows her so little, we have to infer from the dialogue that her attitude toward him moves from friendly politeness (14-36) to taking him quite seriously (37-40) to trying to end the conversation tactfully (41-52) to her final, brutal candor (54-56).

4. By using the third person, Updike is able to achieve greater detachment from his protagonist than would have been possible if William had told his own story. The first-person point of view would have been more limiting, for the third-person allows Updike to show not only what William sees but what he is unable to see.

5. William has been sheltered by the school, with its almost ritually prescribed order, from the chaos of the outside world, and particularly from the risks and pain of close relationships.

6. In effect he puts the episode and his feelings about it behind him, symbolically shutting them up in his locker, feeling "so clean and free he smiled" (59). This, and the following, concluding sentence, confirms the shallowness of his feeling for Mary and his pleasure at returning to the shelter of the school and his scholarly ambitions.

Writing Topics (p. 74)

1. Students will probably be sharply split, with some hating school (or at least professing to hate school) and others--a minority--honest enough to say they enjoy at least parts of school: if not the studies, at least the socializing, club activities, or sports. Taking a wider view by relating their current experiences and feelings to the future path of their lives or careers might be somewhat new to them, especially if, like William, many see school as a place to "hide out" or put off making important decisions. Students might also reflect on how their feelings toward education changed as they grew older and moved from one school to the next.

2. Responses will probably be quite different. Students might be asked, in this case, not to share their essays but to write instead as if confiding to a journal. This should lead to greater sincerity in their writing. If they do share their responses, you might point out how age, ethnicity, religion, gender, family experiences, and careerism influence opinions on love.

3. The clinical nature of this exercise may help students be more frank with themselves because of the distance a textbook will offer. This could turn into a good opportunity for writing that combines technical information with intimate emotions.

Salvation

Langston Hughes

Questions for Study and Discussion (p. 77)

    1. Langston expects to be saved because his aunt and the other townspeople had built up the expectation during the weeks of preparation for the revival meeting.
    In paragraph 3 we see the various appeals made by the preacher, and the preacher's appeals are reinforced by the prayers and songs of the congregation.
    2. The various pressures include:
        a. his Auntie Reed
        b. the community
        c. the preacher
        d. the congregation
        e. other children (Westley in particular)
        f. it was getting late
        g. he was the only one who had not been saved
    When Langston realizes that "God had not struck Westley dead for taking his name in vain or for lying in the temple" (11), he feigns salvation.
    3. He cries because he couldn't tell his aunt that he had lied to everybody in church and that now he didn't believe in Jesus anymore.
    Auntie Reed thinks that he is crying because the Holy Ghost had come into his life and he had seen Jesus.
    The disparity in their views can be attributed to the difference between youth and age, between the literal and the figurative.
    4. Hughes presents the paradox of being saved and yet not really being saved.
    He startles and interests the reader with the paradox. The reader, wishing to learn how the paradox is resolved, reads on.
    5. The third sentence, a typical story opening, serves to introduce the story proper.
    6. The short sentence in paragraph 2 is used for emphasis. The preacher's short sentences in paragraph 3 are used to increase tension and suspense. The long sentence in paragraph 15 lends weight and substance to Hughes's learning experience.
    The short paragraphs (5, 9, and 12) are focal points in the narrative.
    7. Hughes shows us the characters of Auntie Reed, the minister, and Westley through their speech.

8. Some of the words Hughes uses to remind us that we are at a revival meeting are <u>sin</u>, <u>mourners' bench</u>, <u>preached</u>, <u>sermon</u>, <u>hell</u>, <u>prayed</u>, <u>Jesus</u>, <u>congregation</u>, <u>wail</u>, and so forth.

Yes, Hughes uses traditional religious figures of speech such as:
    a. "to bring the young lambs to the fold" (1)
    b. "when you were saved you saw a light" (2)
    c. "lower lights are burning" (4)
    d. "all the new young lambs were blessed in the name of God" (14)

9. Hughes italicizes the word for emphasis. He expected literally to see Jesus, whereas his aunt used the word figuratively--that is, meaning to "see . . . Jesus in your soul."

<u>Writing Topics (p. 77)</u>

1. Before students begin this writing activity, they should review the following aspects of the narrative process: context, selection of details, organization, and point of view.

2. Coming to grips with religious beliefs is just one process where children often find themselves suffering through their difficulties alone as they try to sort out all the conflicting information and emotions. To generate ideas for this writing topic, discuss with students what other issues children generally have to struggle through on their own, and try to establish why these issues are so sensitive. Learning about sex might be a good example with which to begin your discussion.

3. As a prewriting activity for this assignment, have students consider the storylines from movies or television shows they've seen recently, and see if they can come up with some good examples of where seemingly trivial events led to important discoveries. Television sitcoms, in particular, frequently use this type of narrative structure. Your analysis of a few examples may help get students started on examples from their own experiences.

Once More to the Lake

E. B. White

<u>Questions for Study and Discussion (p. 84)</u>

1. The first three paragraphs set the tone and theme for the essay. In the first paragraph White notes the special nature of the Maine lake ("none of us ever thought there was any place in the world like that lake in Maine") and contrasts it with the saltwater he usually sees. In the second paragraph White introduces his son, an important point since the essay largely

concerns their relationship. He also introduces the equally important theme of time: "I wondered how time would have marred this unique, this holy spot." In the third paragraph, White gives the dominant impression of the lake itself, "infinitely remote and primeval" to a child's eye but not completely "wild."

2. Almost everything at the Maine lake remains the same. The same dragonflies seem to hover around the fishing rods; the waves and the boat are just the same. There is even the "same" man bathing with a cake of soap. The tennis court is unchanged, the store is almost identical, and the thunderstorm is just like the ones White witnessed in his youth. The changes in the road, the waitresses, and the motorboats, however, reveal that the times have indeed been changing, particularly the "unfamiliar nervous sound" of the outboard motors: "This was the note that jarred, the one thing that would sometimes break the illusion and set the years moving" (10).

3. White's identification with his son is prompted by hearing him "sneak quietly out and go off along the shore in a boat" (4), just as White used to do as a boy. The identification persists, and in fact forms the core of the essay. For other instances of that identification, see paragraphs 5 and 11. White's identification with his father is not directly alluded to elsewhere, but the intimation of mortality in paragraph 13 surely connects with it. These identifications help to explain White's intense nostalgia and his desire to relive all the old, remembered experiences.

4. White organizes his description of the thunderstorm chronologically, but gives it distinctiveness and a special tone through the metaphor of the "big scene," the "second-act climax" of an old melodrama. Details of the metaphor include the percussion instruments of a pit band and the spectators high in the balcony seats (formerly called "the gods"), "grinning and licking their chops" at the spectacle. The metaphor reduces the storm to a stage effect and, by so doing, makes it seem, not threatening and awe-inspiring, but familiar and friendly, like all of nature at the lake.

5. White's tone is nostalgic, at times lightly humorous and at times lyrical: "Summertime, oh summertime, pattern of life indelible, the fade-proof lake, the woods unshatterable, the pasture with the sweetfern and the juniper forever and ever, summer without end" (8). A case could be made that the tone is elegiac, for White's surprise and delight that nothing has apparently changed grow out of his knowledge that the world has indeed changed greatly, and he with it.

6. As his son puts on the wet swimming trunks, White, still identifying with him, feels a chill in his own groin, and the sensation shocks him out of his languid reverie and reminds him that many years _have_ passed and brought him nearer to death. In a sense the entire essay, with its insistence that "the years were a mirage" (5), has been preparing for this final surprise, which is foreshadowed by White's "creepy" feeling at the identification with

his father: "I would be in the middle of some simple act, I would be picking up a bait box or laying down a table fork, or I would be saying something, and suddenly it would be not I but my father who was saying the words or making the gesture" (4). This identification reveals the passage of time just as the identification with the son denies it.

<u>Writing Topics (p. 84)</u>

1. The further back in their lives students are able to go in pursuing this exploration, the more they will find that things have changed--not only because more time has passed but because they have grown in mind and body. (One of the authors recently returned to the town where he was a boy and discovered that what he remembered as tall buildings were in fact only a few stories high.) And many will be surprised at the tricks their memories have played, rearranging geography and inventing features of buildings or landscapes that do not exist and never did.

2. This question should call forth a good deal of diversity from a class, but many will have rather conventionalized ideas of what a vacation is for. Vacations can have many different purposes: recreation and relaxation, of course, but also the search for one's roots (as in White's essay), the pursuit of a special interest or hobby, self-improvement, or the fulfillment of a long-held wish.

3. Students may have some difficulty identifying exactly when they became aware of their own mortality, so you might advise them to do some recollecting of memorable incidents from their past to see if the process of remembering leads to a recognition of when this awareness dawned. In the same sense that White writes, "It is strange how much you can remember about places . . . once you allow your mind to return into the grooves which lead back" (2), perhaps an expanding sense of the significance of events and places recalled can also occur.

The Endless Streetcar Ride into the Night, and The Tinfoil Noose

Jean Shepherd

<u>Questions for Study and Discussion (p. 91)</u>

1. In paragraph 9, Shepherd explains: "There are about four times in a man's life, or a woman's, too, for that matter, when unexpectedly, from out of the darkness, the blazing carbon lamp, the cosmic searchlight of Truth shines full upon them. It is how we react to those moments that forever seals our fate." He then goes on to state that the episode in the streetcar when he was fourteen was one such moment for him.

11

Shepherd learns, through his date with Junie Jo, that the perception he has of himself is not shared by those around him, that he is, in fact, "a Blind Date that didn't make it" (49). This is a dawning of the realization that he would inevitably become "eternally part of the accursed, anonymous Audience" (4).

2. Shepherd's narrative begins at paragraph 11. The first ten paragraphs introduce the context and central premise for which the narrative serves as an illustration.

3. The distinction between "Official people" and "just us" lies in how people respond to moments of deep insight into their character. Shepherd suggests that those who simply ignore such moments are the ones who rise to prominence, while "we, the Doomed, caught in the brilliant glare of illumination, see ourselves inescapably for what we are, and from that day on skulk in the weeds, hoping no one else will spot us" (9).

Students' responses to this analysis may vary and they should be encouraged to share their reactions and reasoning.

4. Shepherd's essay seems directed at those who are part, as he is, of that great, anonymous Audience forever separated from "the Big Ones." Shepherd identifies himself with this group throughout the essay, particularly in his use of the pronouns "us" and "we," as in paragraphs 3 and 4, and in his central illustrating example, where he shows his keen awareness of and empathy for those who cannot help but see themselves for what they are.

5. The narrator's blind date and, more specifically, Junie Jo's "marble statue" response to him on the streetcar lead to his moment of insight as he looks to the ceiling of the streetcar and notices the "Do You Offend?" sign. That sign triggers his recognition that _he_ is the blind date, not Junie Jo.

6. In its more literal sense, the "tinfoil noose" refers to Shepherd's silky, silvery, hand-painted tie that he prides himself on as he prepares for his date, but that appears ridiculous, "like some crinkly tinfoil noose," after his moment of recognition. A more figurative reading, and the sense in which it is used in the title, is as a description of the feelings of embarrassment and constriction at his moment of truth, of the suffocating awareness that he is looked on as the blind date that didn't make it.

7. Shepherd's description suggests that he was a cocky, awkward, and obnoxious teenager. The "sartorial brilliance" he notes in paragraph 18, of the electric blue sport coat with wide, drooping shoulders and wide lapels, of the flannel slacks that chafed his armpits and grasped his ankles, of the extravagant blood-red snail tie, and of the wavy hair loaded with Greasy Kid Stuff, creates a classic mental image of the nerd who simply tries too hard to be a regular guy.

The personality traits he mentions reinforce this image: the "usual ribald remarks, feckless boasting, and dirty jokes"; his awkward introduction to Junie Jo's father--"I'm here to pick up some girl"; and his obnoxious eagerness to entertain with his "practiced offhand, cynical, cutting sardonic humor" (33). All in all, Shepherd reveals the type of character that would, indeed, be the blind date that didn't make it.

   8. Some of Shepherd's more effective examples of metaphor and simile include:

"we begin to divide into two streams, all marching together up that long yellow brick road of life, but on opposite sides of the street" (1)

"doomed to exist as an office boy in the Mail Room of Life" (5)

"like a rancid, bitter pill" (7)

"the blazing carbon lamp, the cosmic searchlight of Truth" (9)

"grizzled, hardened, tax-paying beetle" (10)

"made of cellophane. You curl easily and everyone can see through you" (10)

"Life was flowing through me in a deep, rich torrent of Castoria. . . . The first rocks were just ahead . . . I was about to have my keel ripped out on the reef" (11)

"as though you are alone in a rented rowboat, bailing like mad in the darkness with a leaky bailing can" (11)

"symphony of sartorial brilliance" (18)

"like vast, drooping eaves" (18)

"Pregnant with Girldom" (20)

"like a broken buzz saw" (21)

"this blinding, fantastic, brilliant, screaming blue light. I am spread-eagled in it. There's a pin sticking through my thorax" (42)

"like bowling balls with laces" (46)

"like some crinkly tinfoil noose" (46)

"The marble statue" (50)

These examples of figurative language establish the tone for the essay. Shepherd's humorous, often bizarre, use of metaphor and simile creates a lighthearted tone, yet the ideas they convey also demonstrate a genuine awareness of an awkward and crucial moment in his life.

Writing Topics (p. 91)

1. As a prewriting activity you can tie in a discussion of study question 3 above with the assignment of this topic. An analysis of how students feel about Shepherd's distinction between "Us and Them," may help them put their own experiences into a perspective that will serve as the focus for their essays.

2. See writing topic 1 above. In addition, for class discussion of this topic, you might focus on some examples of public figures from government, business, and entertainment to see if you can decide whether they do, in fact, reflect Shepherd's assertion about the insensitivity of "Official people."

Learning to See

Samuel H. Scudder

Questions for Study and Discussion (p. 95)

1. As Scudder reveals in paragraphs 25, the best entomological lesson he ever received was Professor Agassiz's repeated injunction to simply "look, look, look." From it Scudder learned the inestimable value of "observing facts and their orderly arrangement" (27) and then bringing them "into connection with some general law" (28).

2. Agassiz's method forces the student to depend on his own initiative and capacity to see in making discoveries and then placing them within the wider context of their applications to science and nature. It works with Scudder because of his innate sense of curiosity and his strong desire to find answers that will satisfy himself and his instructor.

Students' opinions on whether such a method of teaching would be effective today will depend on the degree to which they believe students in general are inquisitive and self-motivated.

3. Scudder studied haemulons for eight months, an amount of time necessary for the slow process of observation and review described in the essay. Students' opinions on whether the process could have been speeded up with the use of lectures or textbooks may vary. Many may allow that it could have been done faster, but to an ultimately less comprehensive and less effective outcome.

4. Scudder hits upon the idea of drawing the fish only after exhausting what he then felt were all other possibilities in simply looking at it. When he does draw it, though, he begins to discover new features as the process of

drawing focuses his attention and concentration more closely to what he is observing. This kind of sharpening of the powers of observation is what Agassiz refers to when he says "a pencil is one of the best eyes."

5. Though Scudder looks back on his first encounter with Professor Agassiz as the most important entomological lesson he ever had, when he was actually experiencing it he was not too pleased. Words and phrases that contribute to this sense of displeasure include: aversion, disappointment, did not commend itself to an ardent entomologist (8); I had seen all that could be seen, lingering, this little excitement over, nothing was to be done, loathsome, ghastly, despair, infinite relief, I was free (9); hideous, feeling of desperation, nonsense (10); piqued, mortified (16); disconcerting, perplexities (20).

Overall, the style and diction of Scudder's essay are formal and academic, and are apparent right away in the first paragraph. Though such style and diction are appropriate for the subject matter, the level of formality does, at times, suggest that the essay was written in the previous century. The following samples of diction are the most obvious clues to the essay's age: my antecedents, purposed (1); eau-de-Cologne (8); interdicted (10).

6. Agassiz's statement suggests that there is no real reason to "look, look, look" and digest or record the results of such observation unless those results can teach you something about general principles of science and nature; otherwise you will simply be filling your head with useless information.

Writing Topics (p. 96)

1. As a prewriting activity you can tie discussion of this topic to consideration of study question 2 above. By looking closely at the approach Professor Agassiz uses to teach Scudder "to see," and then discussing whether such a method would work as well today, students may be better prepared to analyze the influence that an effective teacher has had on them, and how that influence was affected by their own levels of inquisitiveness and ambition.

2. To demonstrate how the pencil can act as one of the best of eyes, you can ask students to do a ten- to fifteen-minute freewriting session in which they respond to Professor Agassiz's or Anne Morrow Lindbergh's comment. When they've finished writing, have them read their responses aloud and then discuss with them what, if anything, they discovered about writing and its relationship to thinking as a result of this short freewriting exercise. 3. This topic will doubtless provoke a lively debate over educational methods, such as quizzes and multiple-choice exams. The fact is, however, that in much of life people are required to answer others' questions, whether a superior's about the reason for declining widget production or a child's about the beginning of the universe, and in this

respect answering the teachers' questions is practice for real life. There are also, of course, many fields in which students learn how to ask questions, fields ranging from the sciences to philosophy, and all subjects have their own methodologies that, among other things, define what kinds of questions are relevant and answerable using the methods of the discipline. The discussion might be turned to this area by asking students what majors or careers they have in mind and what role question-asking plays in those majors and careers.

The Road Not Taken

Robert Frost

Questions for Study and Discussion (p. 98)

1. In line 8 Frost writes that the speaker chose the grassier and less worn path, perhaps believing it offered a fresher, more adventurous experience. That it was a difficult choice is apparent in lines 2 and 3 when the speaker says, I was "sorry I could not travel both / And be one traveler."
The speaker considers the appearance of each path before choosing, and after deciding, consoles himself with the thought that he has "kept the first for another day!" He also recognizes, though, that such returns rarely come to pass.

2. Though the speaker recognizes the importance of his decision and its impact on his life, there is no way for him to know if it was the right decision, since he does not know where the other path might have led him.

3. The yellow wood signifies the entire compass of a person's life, and the diverging roads the choices that need to be made at various points within that compass, choices that determine the specific nature of an individual's life.

4. Frost suggests that regardless of the choices made at such turning points, a person is always left wondering what might have been, and whether the road chosen was the "right" one.
Students may have a variety of good examples to offer that illustrate how decisions made at turning points can affect individual fates.

Writing Topics (p. 98)

1. Students should probably recognize how each author attributes significance to specific moments in a person's life, moments that, though seemingly minor or trivial when they occur, come to have profound effects in the future.
The major difference between the two works is that while Frost suggests that there is no way of knowing whether the right decision has been made,

Hughes conveys a strong sense that he made the wrong decision when he lied about being saved by Jesus.

2. Students should look over the other poems that appear in <u>Outlooks and Insights</u> to help them formulate their opinions about poetry, and perhaps to discover elements they can use to support whatever attitudes they wish to convey in their essays.

3. As a prewriting activity you can discuss with students their decision to attend the college or university in which they are enrolled. Find out what other options were available to them and what implications they might foresee had they chosen any of them. You can also consider whether the possibility of going back and pursuing another path remains open for them, or when, if ever, they think that possibility would no longer be available.

The Story of an Hour

Kate Chopin

<u>Questions for Study and Discussion (p. 101)</u>

1. Mrs. Mallard's friends and relatives believe that her affection for her husband is so strong that she might suffer a heart attack at the news of his death. In truth she experiences a range of feelings from grief to regret to a sense of great freedom. Chopin clearly demonstrates Mrs. Mallard's feelings in her description of her physical symptoms and her innermost thoughts.

2. Chopin uses the following words and phrases to create her sensual expression: "paralyzed inability," "wild abandonment," "storm of grief," "roomy armchair," "delicious breath of rain," "whose lines bespoke repression," "her bosom rose and fell tumultuously," "coursing blood," exalted perception," "her fancy was running riot," "feverish triumph," and "goddess of Victory." This language creates an environment in which the character, the room, and even the weather combine to paint an emotional picture of the emerging individual. The language quickens as Mrs. Mallard's excitement builds.

3. Mrs. Mallard fights her feelings of joy both from guilt and the recognition that such feelings are not socially appropriate for a grieving spouse. She realizes that such independence is not supposed to be desirable to women of her time.

4. Sometimes the best way to argue a point is through subtle example. The narrative form more effectively draws in the reader through its use of imagery that conveys emotion, tension, immediacy, and surprise. In Chopin's time an essay might have been regarded as too bold.

5. Chopin wants her readers to consider her heroine as she considers herself, as lacking any identity other than wife to Mr. Mallard, so that we

may witness her emergence more powerfully. It is only after she has herself experienced her freedom that we hear her sister call her by name through the door.

6. Irony is conveying something different than the true meaning of a word, phrase, or concrete being. The irony of Chopin's story is that Louise died, not from grief at the news of her husband's death, but from disappointment at his being alive.

7. An hour is but a fraction of one's life, yet Louise lived and died a lifetime in that brief time. She was saddened by grief, reborn with hope, and died of disappointment.

Writing Topics (p. 102)

1. In a class discussion you may attempt to discern students' perceptions of the women's movement. Obviously, any students who have had experience with marriage will have a different perspective on this topic. After students have finished this assignment, it may be worthwhile to look over the essays with the class to see if there are any differences between those essays that are merely speculation and those that are based on personal experience, and those written by males and females.

2. This essay may teach the students something about themselves as they take a look at their own relationships. It is important to remind students that they must not only tell but also show by providing incidents and details to illustrate emotions and what leads to these feelings.

Family Ties

Our Son Mark

S. I. Hayakawa

Questions for Study and Discussion (p. 111)

　　1. According to the social worker, caring for Mark at home would put a serious strain on the family and deprive the other children of the love they needed. Hayakawa sums up Mark's actual effect on the family in paragraph 6: "Mark's contentment has been a happy contribution to our family, and the challenge of communicating with him, of doing things we can all enjoy, has drawn the family together. And seeing Mark's communicative processes develop in slow motion has taught me much about the process in all children." As a result of taking care of Mark, the Hayakawa children show a general readiness to understand people and are unusually sensitive, patient, and flexible.

　　2. Hayakawa wrote this essay to persuade his readers that while institutional care may be best for some retarded children, others may be cared for at home to the benefit of the entire family. Underlying this is the more general point that people should be treated as individuals, not as generalizations.

　　3. Hayakawa says in paragraph 9 that his and his wife's "general semantics," as well as their parental feelings, made them aware that the professionals were responding to Mark as a generalization, not as an individual. Moreover, in paragraph 15 Hayakawa notes that his wife was able to recognize a logical flaw in the social worker's question: "Don't your other children live on love, too?"

　　4. The Dark Ages, or Middle Ages, are often cited vaguely as a time of ignorance and superstition, but here the reference is specific: In medieval times the insane and abnormal were almost invariably shut away for life.

　　5. Hayakawa's insistence that it was almost always easy to be patient with Mark may cause some readers to feel that he is glossing over difficulties and presenting an unrealistically positive view of caring for a retarded child. His only qualification of that view is in paragraph 43.

Writing Topics (p. 111)

　　1. In reporting the expert's advice, the students should attempt to recall that advice as precisely as possible, as well as indicating any words,

attitudes, or gestures that may have led them to reject that advice. It would be instructive to review paragraphs 12 to 18 to see how Hayakawa manages this.

2. Students will probably need to research this topic before writing. You might also see if any of your students have information to offer in regard to Down's syndrome as a result of their own encounters in it.

3. We have deliberately supplied an unusable thesis here--that the American family is "in trouble." A discussion of this that leads to some more specific and supportable theses will give students useful practice with this essential skill before approaching their assignment.

My Grandmother: A Rite of Passage

Anthony Brandt

Questions for Study and Discussion (p. 118)

1. "Life is savage, then, and even character is insecure," says Brandt in paragraph 14, after witnessing his grandmother's decline into senility. Yet his mother's similar degeneration has changed his attitude from initial bitterness to acceptance and a kind of wisdom (16). His mother's cheerfulness, despite everything, has helped reconcile him to what has happened to her-- and, we can infer from the last sentences, changed "the color of all [his] expectations" (13).

2. In paragraph 1 Brandt writes: "It felt like and perhaps was the equivalent of a puberty rite: dark, frightening, aboriginal, an obscure emotional exchange between old and young." Though watching his grandmother's deterioration indeed initiated Brandt into one of the responsibilities (and terrors) of adulthood, the experience differed from traditional initiations in that it was solitary, not collective, and was not a performed rite but an extended life experience.

3. Brandt's grandmother experiences a "rite of passage" when she becomes senile, as does Brandt's mother. The family's efforts to ensure that the grandmother was not wakened, the weekend visits to the nursing home, and the author's ministrations to his mother in the final paragraph seem almost ritualistic.

4. Brandt's grandmother is senile for slightly more than a year before she dies, with "a few months" (10) spent in her own home, six months in Brandt's (12), and somewhat more than six months in various nursing homes (13). Brandt says that his grandmother's decline into senility was "rapid" (11); however, his meticulous depiction of the changes in her makes the period seem much longer, so that it seems to encompass his entire childhood.

5. Many students will choose the description of the grandmother's senility in paragraph 11, which is painfully graphic. The paragraph begins with a forcefully blunt topic sentence and proceeds with disturbances in the family's life. Besides the grotesque details, note the insistent repetition of the words she and calling. Something of Brandt's state of mind at the time comes through when he says he sometimes took fifteen minutes to close the garage door silently so as not to awaken his grandmother.

6. "Sensibilities" here means responsiveness to others' feelings; the transformation of his grandmother from a loved and loving person to a feared and demanding caricature of herself is a form of "violence," a "violation" of the boy's feelings. The words suggest an analogy with rape, also the perversion of something that normally expresses loving feelings.

Writing Topics (p. 119)

1. An essential element of this question is describing the grandparents and their activities to provide support for general observations and conclusions. In answering the last part of the question, students might try imagining themselves in turn as children, parents, and grandparents, so that they may grasp the complex interrelationships involved.

2. Thoughtful students will find that this assignment juxtaposes a stereotype (their conception of "old age") with numerous "examples" who don't fit the mold. In fact, apart from the physiological effects of aging, old people are as diverse as people of any other age or class. For students who don't get the point, an exchange of papers and class discussion should put it across.

A Tale of Two Gravies

Karen P. Engelhardt

Questions for Study and Discussion (p. 123)

1. Engelhardt's grandmothers were alike in that they both hosted almost ritualistic dinners and were family matriarchs. They taught her similar lessons about commitment and the importance of family ties and support. They were different in personality: Grandma Ruth was talkative and very American, Grandma Meatball was quieter and "Old World Italian." As a child, Engelhardt saw only the differences; when she grew older, she understood that they actually had much in common and that their similarities were more important.

2. The gravies symbolize the differences between her grandmothers that stood out in Engelhardt's mind when she was a little girl. The use of the

word "gravy" links her grandmothers, even though their gravies were different and they had different personalities.

    3. The fact that the family consistently visited both grandmothers illustrates how Engelhardt's parents were committed to fostering their relationship with their mothers, even after growing up and raising their own family. They evidently learned the lessons taught by their mothers. Besides the food, family stories and lore were passed along. According to Engelhardt, it is this family lore and her grandmothers' examples of love that make up their legacy to her.

    4. Engelhardt has learned that what on the surface may appear different is actually alike on a more fundamental plane. Her grandmothers' roles in keeping their families together were something they shared, even though they communicated that message in unique ways. It is this message that Engelhardt now considers their lasting contribution to her development; passing that message on to her own family constitutes her duty as an adult.

Writing Topics (p. 123)

    1. This assignment will yield different results from various students. Because of this diversity, they should be encouraged to share their essays with each other. The essays can be both positive and negative, including both fond recollections of good days and difficult recollections of hackneyed rituals devoid of real meaning. This kind of memory task might also produce some deep feelings that should be addressed in the essay as well.

    2. Besides the comparison of content, students might consider how males and females remember their grandparents: Are there things they both recall, or do men focus on one kind of memory and women on another? Do men and women react to old age differently? Do younger and older people?

Those Winter Sundays

Robert Hayden

Questions for Study and Discussion (p. 125)

    1. The speaker, who has always taken his father's morning chores for granted, now realizes that they were actually gestures of love. That his father performed them on winter Sundays "too" is an act of particular selflessness, for on those days the father could have slept late.

    2. "The chronic angers of that house" is an oblique and indeed vague expression; nothing in the poem reveals who was angry at whom or what. Students' answers to this question will doubtless be more specific than the

text permits, and this can be used to start a useful class discussion on accurate reading.

3. Most children--and many young people--simply do not realize how much easier their lives have been made by their parents' labor and sacrifices. And it also happens frequently that children are indifferent to or even fearful of loving parents who cannot show their feelings.

4. The speaker is anguished by his childhood insensitivity. The repetition of the phrase "what did I know" communicates that emotion.

5. Hayden's diction varies between the direct ("No one ever thanked him") and the formal ("love's austere and lonely offices"). The variation points up the contrast between the ordinary, everyday activities with which the father demonstrated his love and the deeper significance the speaker now finds in those activities. The tone likewise varies from the matter-of-fact to the ceremonial, and for the same purpose.

6. Offices in this context suggests both "an act performed for another, usually beneficial" (American Heritage Dictionary) and, from the connotations of austere, a ceremony or rite as in a church. Students might be encouraged to look up the word in their dictionaries and see which other definitions fit and develop the sense of the line, and of the poem's theme.

Writing Topics (p. 125)

1. In preparation for this exercise, students might be invited to consider motivations for "loving" actions other than love--a sense of duty or responsibility, for example--and also the fact that actions arising from love may harm the loved one.

2. In writing about causes and effects, students should keep in mind the requirement that a cause or causes must be both sufficient and necessary to bring about a purported effect. Such tests can seldom be applied to one's own experience or one's impressions of others, at least as regards the development of behavior patterns, and so any students who wish to go beyond a personal essay on family incidents and the resulting feelings should be encouraged to do some reading in the behavioral sciences--as the end of this question suggests.

Heritage

Linda Hogan

Questions for Study and Discussion (p. 127)

1. Since Hogan writes in the greatest detail about her grandmother, the reader may assume that she is most indebted to her. The lines about the

grandmother are the most descriptive. From her grandmother, she learns of her connections to the Oklahoma land and her Chickasaw heritage. Her grandmother passes on the stoic wisdom, medicine, and understanding of her tribe. From her--and the rest of the family--Hogan has learned the "secrets" of life.

2. Hogan seems to enjoy the antique mirror from her mother, but not the fact that she sees her face aging in it; the smell of baking bread is also a fond memory. Her eyes are from her father, and the wood that reminds her of her childhood homes comes from her uncle. Hogan seems ambivalent about her grandparents' legacies to her.

3. It seems that someone or some institution--the U.S. government, maybe--did not want her tribe to continue living in their traditional ways. Continuing to sing the old chants was one way the Chickasaw tribe could maintain its identity. Because her father "was told not to remember," he seems to have been prevented from carrying on his ancestral traditions.

4. The whiteness of her shirt stands for the color of her skin: lighter than the traditional tones of her Chickasaw ancestors. She has therefore been integrated to some degree into mainstream culture and this has, in consequence, put distance between her and her roots.

5. Whenever a poet does this, he or she is making a substantive point in a stylistic manner: This separation indicates an important moment in the poem.

The images of brown and black indicate a certain connection with nature that was part of her tribe's experiences: food, soil, and medicine that gave them power. These were important aspects of her relatives' lives. Her grandmother's snuff and the use of dark colors link her with the past, even while her grandmother herself may not have been a full Chickasaw, as indicated by her blue eyes. The phrase "tobacco is the dark night that covers me" illustrates that the past is never far from the author's experiences, but that this past is associated in her mind with protection.

6. Hogan sounds matter-of-fact in recognizing the various strands of her heritage. In the end Hogan believes that her heritage and the people from whom she derived it are far more important than "having a home."

<u>Writing Topics (p. 128)</u>

1. Students might begin by listing those things they contribute to their families and those things they take from them. They can then distinguish between these qualities and consider where they fit in to their families in the past and where they currently stand. Has their position changed over time? Students who have had to take a more adult or leadership role at home, particularly financially, may find this assignment especially challenging and revealing.

2. Instead of considering the family as a whole (which will work for

some students), perhaps choosing the most memorable character--an uncle, perhaps, or a parent--who may have been colorful, eccentric, outstanding, or the like, will help students identify and discuss formative people and events. Students can then try to paint a verbal picture of the character or event.

3. Before committing their thoughts to paper, students would probably benefit from discussing the generation gap that exists between them and their parents and, to go one step deeper, the one that stood between their parents and grandparents. This will give them a sense of their family's ongoing history. Can they detect certain values, customs, and beliefs that have persisted, albeit in varying forms, that have remained constant within their families over two or three generations? This question will enable students to wrestle with the task of distinguishing between the form of a family custom and its emotional content.

A Worn Path

Eudora Welty

<u>Questions for Study and Discussion (p. 136)</u>

1. Phoenix is going to the hospital in Natchez to obtain medicine for her grandson's throat, which had been burned two or three years previously when he swallowed lye (91). She tells nobody the nature of her journey; one of the nurses at the hospital knows why she has come and asks about her grandson. Phoenix has been so preoccupied with walking to Natchez that she forgot her purpose (90).

2. Along the way Phoenix encounters a long uphill path, a thorn bush, a log across a creek, a barbed wire fence, a "maze" in the woods, a scarecrow that she mistakes for a ghost, an alligator swamp, a black dog, a deep ditch, a hunter who points a gun at her, and, finally, the bewildering city. She overcomes each obstacle with determination, dignity, and good humor, talking to herself for moral support. See, for example, her reaction to the thorn bush in paragraph 8. Her indomitable nature is suggested by her name, Phoenix, evoking the mythical bird that lives five hundred years and then is reborn from its own ashes.

3. Phoenix recovers the first nickel after it drops from the hunter's pocket (49, 54) and craftily coaxes the second one from the hospital nurse (99). She plans to use the money to buy a paper windmill for her grandson for Christmas (103). The gift, like Phoenix's journey, reveals the depth of her self-sacrificing love for the boy.

4. Phoenix and her grandson depend on each other for survival. The grandson needs the medicine Phoenix pursues in her treks to Natchez, while

Phoenix's life rests on the fulfillment of this mission. Both roles contribute to the sustaining bond of love between them.

5. The Surrender is the end of the Civil War. Phoenix Jackson evidently grew up as a slave, and slaves did not have the opportunity to go to school.

6. In paragraph 1 Welty describes Phoenix as swaying from side to side "with the balanced heaviness and lightness of a pendulum in a grandfather clock." Her wrinkled skin looks "as though a whole little tree stood in the middle of her forehead" (2); she climbs the hill "like a baby trying to climb the steps" (16) and lies on her back "like a June-bug waiting to be turned over" (39). Taken together these images suggest that old Phoenix is like a force of nature, enduring and indomitable.

7. Literally, the title refers to the path Phoenix has walked again and again to Natchez. The larger significance is best suggested by Welty herself in paragraph 10 of the essay "Is Phoenix Jackson's Grandson Really Dead?": "What I hoped would come clear was that in the whole surround of this story, the world it threads through, the only certain thing at all is the worn path. The habit of love cuts through confusion and stumbles or contrives its way out of difficulty, it remembers the way even when it forgets, for a dumbfounded moment, its reason for being. The path is the thing that matters." This would be an appropriate point at which to discuss Welty's comments in that essay on the overall meaning of her story.

8. Welty has written an essay on this subject entitled "Is Phoenix Jackson's Grandson Really Dead?" In paragraph 6 of that essay Welty sums up her answer: "To the question 'Is the grandson really dead?' I could reply that it doesn't make any difference. I could also say that I did not make him up in order to let him play a trick on Phoenix. But my best answer would be: 'Phoenix is alive!'" The point of the story then turns not on the fate of the grandson but on Phoenix's journey itself, as the rest of Welty's essay makes clear. Many readers seem to feel that Phoenix's refusal to believe that her grandson is dead would emphasize her indomitable spirit. Phoenix's puzzling silence after the hospital nurse asks why she has come leads some readers to speculate that Phoenix may have for a moment remembered the grandson's death, instead of having simply forgotten the reason for her errand. In addition the somewhat allegorical quality of the story may prompt readers to search for deeper meanings. But in fact the story does not provide any basis for such an interpretation.

Writing Topics (p. 136)

1. The descriptions should not only convey as exact a picture as possible but should also create a clear dominant impression. Students should use precise language and, where appropriate, figurative language. Welty's story is a stimulating and usable model.

2. Preparation for this exercise should include consideration of both

general obligations--those all fathers, mothers, or children share--and the particulars of each student's situation. The underlying topic here is the nature of responsibility and its sources in individuals and groups.

3. Students usually enjoy reading more of Welty. In reading other stories and essays by Welty they will find that her treatment of Phoenix Jackson is typical of her sympathetic, appreciative, and accurate treatment of African-American people throughout her work.

The Troubled American Family

Can the American Family Survive?

Margaret Mead

Questions for Study and Discussion (p. 146)

1. In paragraph 3 Mead states that "very young couples, the poorly educated, those with few skills and a low income, [and] Blacks and members of other minority groups" are more prone to breakdowns within the family. The communication and economic pressures commonly associated with these groups create instability in relationships and often lead to divorce.

The effect of this breakdown on children of "secure" families is stated in paragraph 4: "How can children feel secure when their friends in other families so like their own are conspicuously lost and unhappy?"

2. Mead outlines the consequences of family breakdown in paragraphs 12 to 20. The effects on adults include: (1) large numbers of young couples repudiating or delaying marriage and simply living together, "dependent on their private, personal commitment to each other for the survival of their relationship" (12); (2) growing numbers of men and women "who have outlived their slender family relationships" and are forced to depend on public institutions (13); and (3) increasing demands that women join the work force, not always out of a desire to do so, but because they must to survive economically (14).

The effect on children is even more desperate, according to Mead: (1) large numbers of adolescent runaways, particularly young girls (17); (2) children "discovering the obliterating effects of alcohol" (18); (3) young girls and boys wandering the streets, often falling victim to "corruption and sordid sex" (18); and (4) a "vast increase in child abuse" (19).

3. The most alarming symptom of family trouble, in Mead's view, is the "vast increase in child abuse" (19). She believes "that frantic mothers and fathers, stepparents or the temporary mates of parents turn on the children they do not know how to care for, and beat them--often in a desperate,

inarticulate hope that someone will hear their cries and somehow bring help" (19).

4. The following explanations for the breakdown of family life are offered in the essay:

1. the movement from rural areas and small towns to the big cities, and the movement from one part of the country to another
2. the effect of unemployment and underemployment among minority groups
3. the generation gap
4. failure to provide for children and young people "whom we do not succeed in educating, who are in deep trouble and who may be totally abandoned" (25)
5. the problem of hard drugs
6. parental permissiveness and lack of discipline
7. Women's Liberation

Students' responses to these explanations will vary. As you discuss them, you may also wish to find out their reactions to the "panaceas" mentioned in paragraphs 29 and 30.

5. Mead does not advocate returning to the past. Instead, she explains that looking to the past "can provide us only with a base for judging what threatens sound family life and for considering whether our social planning is realistic and inclusive enough" (39). In acting thus, Mead believes we will be better able to find "new solutions in keeping with our deepest human needs" (39).

6. Mead's concern in this statement is that we have tried too hard to isolate individual families from the community at large and, as a result, have encouraged the separation of generations and the break from a sense of home community. This has placed a much larger burden on every small family because they have taken over responsibilities formerly shared among three generations and within the community.

7. By dividing her introduction into five paragraphs, Mead helps delineate the separate ideas discussed in them. The bold print subheading-- "The Grim Picture"--then identifies the start of the body of the essay for readers. Though combining paragraphs 1 through 5 into one may have created a better sense of introduction, it would also have jumbled the ideas together, making them less distinguishable and, ultimately, less effective in introducing what follows.

8. Mead begins her discussion of possible solutions by stating: "Both optimism and action are needed." She then offers the following:

1. support federal legislation intended to help provide for families in need

28

2. support federal programs for day care and afterschool care; for centers for the elderly where they won't be isolated; for housing for young families and older people so they can interact; for a national health program; and for "family impact" requirements on government agency policies
3. realize that "problems related to family and community life . . . are interlocked" and that "we need awareness of detail combined with concern for the whole, and a wise use of tax dollars to accomplish our aims" (50)
4. accept the idea that each of us "shares in the responsibility for everyone" (51)
5. support communities where there is housing for three generations, for the fortunate and unfortunate, and for people of many backgrounds (52)
6. "interrupt the runaway belief that marriages must fail, that parents and children can't help but be out of communication, that the family as an institution is altogether in disarray" through nationwide discussion (53)

There can be extensive class discussion on any of these proposed solutions.

Mead does not see the dissolution of the family structure as an easier solution simply because there are still far more successful marriages and child-parent relationships than there are failures.

Writing Topics (p. 146)

1. An in-depth discussion of study questions 4 and 8 above may lead students to consider some more innovative alternatives to the family as the central social unit in our society. You can also look at the alternatives mentioned in paragraph 29 of the essay and explore the possibilities of each in more detail.

2. It may be interesting to discuss, as a class, the extent to which students' families have been isolated from the interaction of generations, as well as from the larger society. Find out if there is any evidence in students' experiences that the single-family unit has taken on the responsibilities "once shared within three generations and among a large number of people--the nurturing of small children, the emergence of adolescents into adulthood, the care of the sick and disabled and the protection of the aged" (42). Your discussion may also help students draw conclusions about the importance of their families in their own lives.

Homosexuality: One Family's Affair

Michael Reese and Pamela Abramson

Questions for Study and Discussion (p. 153)

    1. Kelly's parents did not "know" their son because they could only imagine what his life-style consisted of. For them "knowing" their son involved certain expectations for his future including a wife and children and a traditional life-style.

    2. The stereotypes of homosexual men led Kelly to believe that if he were himself homosexual, he had to be perverted, limp-wristed, and effeminate. Kelly was not these things and so was unsure of his sexuality. All he was sure of was that he did not like girls, "faggot" jokes, or postgame drinking. Having no positive gay role models in his life he could not acknowledge his homosexuality.

    3. Gay men, as Kelly first believed, were pornographic, effeminate, and perverted--aging drag queens. When he finally went to a gay bar he realized they were "average Joes," not physically different from heterosexuals, and that they had families, careers, and everyday lives.

    4. Kelly strove to be a perfectionist so that no one would be able to find fault with him. He was a teacher's pet, good at football, and a member of many social groups.

    5. All the members of the family asked themselves, "Why Kelly?" Kelly didn't have the answer, as his parents thought he would, nor did he choose his life-style. Everyone, including Kelly, felt horror at his homosexuality. Kelly's parents also experienced guilt over what they must have "done wrong" in raising him. Joan read books and joined support groups in an attempt to get closer to the situation and make sense of it. Paul said he accepted it, but opted for mental storming over participation in parent support groups. He said he realizes he cannot turn his back on his son no matter what Kelly's sexual orientation. Kelly made the decision to express his real feelings rather than suppress them. At first he kept his distance from his family, then he let his parents into his life in hopes that the more it became a reality for them, the more they would be able to accept it. Kelly is doing what he needs to and it seems to be working, as his father is finally a part of his life again. Each member of the family seems to be doing the best they can.

    6. The authors have stayed neutral in reporting the story of the family. When referring to Joan or Paul, the authors do not condemn their initial horror or praise their eventual acceptance of their son, but see both as inevitable. They acknowledge that the situation is equally difficult for Kelly, who is dealing with trying to express his sexuality and at the same time gain acceptance from his family.

7. The Chronisters ask themselves, "Why my son?" "Where did we go wrong?" "What made him like this?" "What's going to happen to him?" "What kind of a life will he have?" The authors do not try to answer questions of why or how, because they want to show the futility of such questions. They emphasize the future rather than the past: his parents' coping strategies, the evolution of Kelly's identity as a gay man, and his concerns for his future.

Writing Topics (p. 153)

1. As a prewriting activity you may conduct a discussion that characterizes each of the family members. Have the students share their perceptions of each member. Once the characterizations have been made, students may find it easier to determine why a particular family member is more sympathetic.
2. It may be important for students to describe the emotion they would feel working up the nerve to tell their parents, and the emotions their parents would feel, rather than just to present a narrative.

All Happy Clans Are Alike: In Search of the Good Family

Jane Howard

Questions for Study and Discussion (p. 162)

1. These qualities are catalogued and discussed in paragraphs 11 through 28. Each good family has a founder or chief around which the family revolves, and an archivist or switchboard operator who keeps track of all the members. Good families are not closed or exclusive groups; they are hospitable and open. In addition, the good family can handle difficulties and is affectionate, albeit in a wide variety of ways. Rituals provide a sense of togetherness, belonging, and place. Good families have some sense of the heritage they will leave behind--namely, their children--and also respect and honor their elders.
2. Howard divides the essay into three main parts, The first, paragraphs 1 to 10, includes a discussion of her thesis, that families can be extended. She also talks about how the need to belong to a family is a basic human desire. The second part, paragraphs 11 to 28, lists and describes the qualities of a good family. The third, paragraphs 29 to 43, offers her concluding observations and thoughts.
3. Friends of the road are met and held by chance: at school or work or in a neighborhood. These relationships often serve an immediate purpose and last only for a relatively brief time. Friendships of the heart, however,

run deeper and longer; they are slower to develop. Friends of the heart must work to make these relationships last over distance and time; they share a history and a full context in which new events take place.

4. The author finds that families today are disconnected and scattered. Careerism leads to more single, childless lives or smaller, more strained families than in the past. Since there is so much activity going on--jobs, traveling, relocating segments of the family--it is difficult to keep the family core intact. Also, biological ties do not necessarily lead to friendships; two different things are at work.

5. Howard draws from personal experiences, stories she has heard, and examples of family life from the United States and beyond. She also uses quotations from famous thinkers (for example, Buber and Kierkegaard) and from literary sources. The most effective examples are those that are most easily pictured in the reader's mind, such as the last two sentences of paragraph 13 or the birthday cake from paragraph 5. The audience can readily identify and empathize with these scenes because they are familiar and common to many people.

6. Howard believes that true familial relationships are forged by time, sweat, tears, hard work, sacrifice, sharing of happiness and sadness, laughter, and tears. Only in such trying circumstances can a friendship be produced that is lasting, significant, and honest.

Writing Topics (p. 163)

1. Students can list their "tribes" before writing, casting as broad a net as possible: home, school (academic, social, and sports groups), clubs, neighborhood, job, and religious organization. They might apply Howard's distinction between friends of the road and friends of the heart when writing about these tribes.

2. These essays should be as descriptive as possible. It might help to suggest that students describe a ritual as if they were writing a movie scene to be filmed. Students might sense that a variety of needs are fulfilled for different people at various stages of their lives by these rituals. Ask them to consider where they themselves have fit in, where they currently fit in, and what they imagine the future to hold for them with regard to a particular family ritual. Some students may feel trapped by these family rituals but may feel a sense of belonging in another tribe--on a sports team, for instance, and during its rituals. Which is more important to them now: their biological family or their tribes?

Paul's Case

Willa Cather

<u>Questions for Study and Discussion (p. 179)</u>

1. Cather uses a direct method of characterization to show how the outer person reflects the inner character. Paul's dress, a bit old and worn but still stylish, indicates that he is concerned with his appearance though unable to afford very much in the way of clothing. His red carnation, under the circumstances, indicates his defiant manner, and his height and eyes illustrate that he is very "alive" and dynamic underneath the surface.

2. In paragraph 3, Paul's teachers complain that he is disorderly and impertinent. They dislike his defiance, his lack of respect for authority, and his distance and inattentiveness in class. The ease with which he lies and his aversion to physical contact indicate a kind of willed isolation from others.

3. Paul eventually withdraws from school and from work at Carnegie Hall. Paul's defiance at the "inquisition" prefigures his attitude later in the story. He has a running conflict with his father that underlies much of the story. He clashes with his teachers and his peers. In the end Paul confronts himself and succumbs to a suicidal impulse.

4. Paul feels trapped, as if he is drowning in a sea of conformity, repression, and hopelessness. He feels he will die if he does not escape the mundane, choking atmosphere. His red carnation stands out sharply when contrasted with the "colorless mass of everyday existence" (19) and it symbolizes how he does not fit into his surroundings and wishes to break away from them.

5. In paragraphs 18 and 32, we learn that Paul wants to be an insider, to belong and be accepted in the artistic world of nonconformity and style, which the concert hall represents. He is comfortable there, but he does not want to be an actor or musician (32); he simply wants to be part of the life surrounding a concert hall (29).

6. If Cather had used a first-person narrative for this short story, it would have been a more intimate and thoughtful account of the incidents. The story would have been less detached, but also less objective and, maybe, more self-righteous as well. Cather wants the reader to get close to Paul, but not to be actually inside his head. Students might debate the merit of her choice, or be asked to rewrite an incident from the story in Paul's voice.

7. This boy is a respectable family man on the rise--everything Paul's father wishes Paul to be but knows he is not. Precisely because the boy is so ordinary, mundane, bland, and unexceptional, Paul dislikes him. The boy is neither what Paul is nor what he wants to be.

8. Paul does appear to be lazy, hopeless, and an impractical dreamer. Some students will find this attractive, while others will show disdain for him. It could be that his case was bad based on the other characters' idea of success. But Paul had different things in mind. He refuses to follow the beaten track. This could well make him honorable in the opinion of some student readers.

9. Again, students' feelings will vary, especially if they have some experience with suicide in their families or circle of friends. Some might think he "copped out" because he felt he could never escape the depression of Cordelia Street. He could have gone back and taken his punishment or he could have continued to drift; this latter option would have been viable given Paul's restlessness and romanticism. Perhaps the revolver "was not the way" because it was not spectacular enough. Paul was a dreamer and probably desired a big finish to his life; at least then his death would have been distinguished.

Writing Topics (p. 180)

1. Many students feel trapped. Depending on where they live and the economic climate of their town and parents, they will feel more or less trapped. Their academic or athletic abilities will also be a factor in their answers, since these abilities might provide a way out for them.

It is difficult for Paul to find a way out because he has no real imagination or creativity that can be applied in a practical way: He is an idealistic dreamer living in a fantasy world.

Students will react strongly to this question of conformity and should be asked to be specific in their complaints and plausible in their alternatives. Most will probably think their lives are harder today than Paul's was at the time of the story. They should be encouraged to think critically about what is common to teenagers' experiences and what is different in different places and times. If students have read essays about nonconformity, such as Thoreau's ideas on civil disobedience or passages from Walden, they might use this other literature to complement their ideas about "Paul's Case."

2. There are little white lies and there are big black lies. Students should be asked to distinguish between them and consider whether lying is an absolute or relative flaw. They should also discuss the difference between lying to themselves and to others: Which has a greater potential for difficulties? Again, specific examples from their own lives will lead to more substantial writing.

What Are Friends?

On Friendship

Margaret Mead and Rhoda Metraux

Questions for Study and Discussion (p. 184)

1. In paragraph 4, Mead and Metraux describe Americans' conception of the term "friend": "[It] can be applied to a wide range of relationships--to someone one has known for a few weeks in a new place, to a close business associate, to a childhood playmate, to a man or woman, to a trusted confidant. There are real differences among these relations for Americans--a friendship may be superficial, casual, situational or deep and enduring." Europeans, though, do not see the differences in these relations and, according to Mead and Metraux, believe that "people known and accepted temporarily, casually, flow in and out of Americans' homes with little ceremony and often with little personal commitment" (5).
Students' reaction to Mead's and Metraux's definition may vary. Those who have traveled abroad may have insights to share in regard to how Europeans view friendship both for themselves and for Americans.

2. The authors' purpose is to explain. This is evident by the statement presented in paragraph 6--"Who, then, is a friend?"--which is repeated in slightly different form in the concluding paragraph--"What, then, is friendship?" Mead and Metraux attempt to arrive at an internationally applicable definition of friendship.

3. According to Mead and Metraux, in France "friendship is a one-to-one relationship that demands a keen awareness of the other persons's intellect, temperament and particular interests. A friend is someone who draws out your own best qualities" (9). French friendships are also compartmentalized--"different friends fill different niches in each person's life" (10). In Germany, "friendship is much more articulately a matter of feeling" and "friendships are based on mutuality of feeling" (13), in contrast to the French inclination toward intellectuality and lively disagreement. Finally, in England the basis for friendship is "shared activity" and usually takes place outside the family (14).
Students' responses to these types of friendship may vary. Some may note how American views on friendship tend to incorporate aspects of all three of the above.

4. Mead and Metraux see the difference between friendship and kinship as the necessity to invoke free choice--"a friend is someone who chooses and is chosen" (15), whereas kinship is a matter of blood relations.

5. In the last sentence of their essay Mead and Metraux state that "the

35

American's characteristic openness to different styles of relationship makes it possible for him to find new friends abroad with whom he feels at home."

<u>Writing Topics (p. 185)</u>

1. In responding to these three questions students will likely incorporate elements of definition, illustration, and process analysis into their essays. It may therefore by helpful to review these patterns of organization and development before they begin. You can also review samples of each as they appear in the other essays on friendship in this section.
2. For different perspectives on the nature of relationships between men and women, you can have students review Marc Feigen Fasteau's "Friendships among Men" (p. 190), Jennifer Crichton's "College Friends" (p. 186), and Susan Jacoby's "Unfair Game" (p. 207). You can also discuss how the possibility of friendship between men and women is affected by how the issue of women's rights is perceived by those involved.

College Friends

Jennifer Crichton

<u>Questions for Study and Discussion (p. 189)</u>

1. Chrichton says the first semester at college is the most difficult time to make friends because it is a lonely time; many people bond together only for brief periods simply because they feel isolated and alienated and are longing for the kind of human contact they had in high school, rather than because their actual chemistry is the stuff of good relationships. Student responses will vary; have them explore how certain relationships fit different patterns and how they think particular relationships will turn out.
2. Crichton believes she was so desperate and starved for intimacy that she spilled out deeply felt emotions and information to the first person she met. In paragraph 2, she uses the word <u>panic</u> to describe her "violent" need for a friend. Now, she cannot even remember that person's name, whom she later passed in a corridor almost without recognition (3).
3. She met her best friend, Jean, by arguing with her in and after a film class about Alfred Hitchcock (5). Their friendship has since followed the pattern of this initial meeting: They have grown closer, but each has strong opinions and tells them pointblank to the other. There is an honesty and directness that they share.
4. Lovers make poor best friends because there are other dynamics at work in that sort of relationship that preclude the utter candor that usually exists between best friends. As Crichton recalls, "Sexual tension charged

36

the lines of communication between us" (7). Students may react against this notion with vehemence, because many believe a person's best friend can indeed be a lover as well. Male and female students may have different perspectives on this issue. Students might also consider whether a best friend can or should be a person of the same gender.

5. Friendships made after college are not as deep or intimate as college friendships, the author writes in paragraph 14. As her friend Pam points out, in college people tend to share their entire lives from dawn to dusk. After college, people encounter each other in passing, at different times of the day, resulting in what Pam calls encounters of "fractions of people." Relationships may be tied up with office politics or careerism, situations in which utter sincerity may not work and in which there is an entirely different atmosphere and agenda.

6. When Crichton visits with college friends, she feels "a certain sense of loss" because the spontaneity of college life has given way to a business rhythm of the day and week (17). She maintains, however, that the importance and value of her friendships have deepened since college. Because students are still in college, they may not be able to empathize. Ask them, then, to consider this question in the context of their high school friendships.

Writing Topics (p. 189)

1. Students may be reluctant to discuss these points and definitions because they may have specific feelings about particular people in the class. This assignment might be better treated as a journal or diary exercise in order to facilitate an honest effort.

2. A prewriting exercise would have students list those qualities that first attracted them to the person, the qualities that have since kept them friends, and how their first impressions matched later experiences. Then the students could write a "history" of the relationship. Since so much of this assignment is descriptive, asking the students to think of it as a personality profile for a magazine feature might help them organize and write.

3. This assignment follows directly from the previous writing topic. If possible, students should be encouraged to share the essay with the person who is its subject. Invite students to speculate as well on how they think the relationship might grow. The issue of lifelong friendship might also be applied to a parent, sibling, or other relative, which brings up the additional factor of the role age plays in such a relationship.

Friendships among Men

Marc Feigen Fasteau

Questions for Study and Discussion (p. 198)

1. As Fasteau explains in paragraph 2, the belief that the great friendships are between men is a myth because usually "something is missing. Despite the time men spend together, their contact rarely goes beyond the external, a limitation which tends to make their friendships shallow and unsatisfying."

2. See question 1 above.

3. In paragraph 12 Fasteau states: "The sources of this stifling ban on self-disclosure, the reasons why men hide from each other, lie in the taboos and imperatives of the masculine stereotype." These taboos and imperatives include the belief that men are supposed to be functional; the obsessive competitiveness that often exists between male friends; and the fear of being or being thought homosexual.

According to Fasteau, men rationalize this fear of intimacy by convincing themselves that only those men whose problems have overwhelmed them--in other words, only weak men--feel the need for self-disclosure and expressiveness.

4. Fasteau believes that games play such an important role in men's lives because they "stave off a lull in which they would be together without some impersonal focus for their attention" (5). Games give men something besides themselves to talk about.

Women also use games as a means for getting together, but "the games themselves are not the only means of communication" (5, note).

5. The exceptions that Fasteau notes when men will become personal are: (1) when they are drunk; (2) when they are talking to strangers; and (3) when they are in a mixed group and can depend on women to facilitate the conversation.

6. Fasteau believes that "competitiveness feeds the most basic obstacle to openness between men, the inability to admit to being vulnerable" (17).

Students' responses to this belief may vary and it may be interesting to note if there are significant differences between male and female responses.

7. This last question can facilitate an open-ended discussion in which you analyze the way male friends are currently portrayed in the media. You can also ask students to consider the cause and effect relationship of this portrayal. Does the media simply reflect attitudes as they already exist? Or does it help establish and foster the way men look at each other as friends?

1. Students may find it helpful to take one aspect of Fasteau's analysis of male friendships and use it as the basis for a refutation. For instance, some may find that his conclusions about the role that games play in male relationships do not allow for the positive effects that games can contribute. An argumentative counteranalysis of games could then demonstrate how such contact does, at times, go beyond the "external."

2. A prewriting discussion in which you generate ideas about why men "hide from each other" and how they might communicate more meaningfully may help students get started on this assignment. One way to approach such a discussion is to consider ways that women differ from men in their ability to communicate with each other, and to speculate on whether these differences could ever be incorporated in male views on friendship.

The Last Day (from Charlotte's Web)

E. B. White

Questions for Study and Discussion (p. 203)

1. Wilbur feels that he is unworthy of all that Charlotte has done for him because he has done nothing for her in return.

2. Charlotte replies, "You have been my friend." To her, friendship is reason enough to want to do things for someone without expecting something in return.

3. White takes human emotions and places them in animals. He makes these emotions so real that readers may even forget that they are reading the story of a friendship between a pig and a spider. By showing the thoughts and emotions through the animals, White emphasizes them; he says, in effect, here are animals with the proper outlook, why can't humans understand all this?

4. Wilbur repays Charlotte by promising to bring her children home with him to the barn, where they can live with him in the place where their mother lived. His motivation is his love for Charlotte and the desire to be there for her children because she is going to die.

5. Templeton has been a friend to both Charlotte and Wilbur; however, he has done so begrudgingly. He has been the object of abuse because by tradition that is the way humans respond to rats. More importantly, Templeton never does anything without considering what's in it for him. White's portrayal of Templeton tells us that these kinds of creatures exist and that if we want their help and cooperation we have to find ways to motivate them. Gratuitous kindness is not their way. Such individuals can't be ignored. We simply have to learn how to live with them.

<u>Writing Topics (p. 203)</u>

1. Students can write about present or past friendships that have meant a great deal to them. They may even explore lost friendships and how they affected them. This may lead to some deeply felt essays, and students should be encouraged not to hide their feelings.

2. This essay can go in a variety of directions. Encourage students to be descriptive no matter who they choose to write about so that a clear picture of the person emerges. Have them focus on characterization, physical description, setting, and illustrative anecdotes.

3. In preparing to write their short tales, students should do the following: a) make sure that they have a very full understanding of what their own definition of friendship is, b) decide who the characters of the story will be, c) decide what the story line itself will be, d) select a conflict or situation in which characters can act out or show this meaning of friendship. In the actual writing of the story, students should be sure to use dialogue to make the story come alive. Have your students read their stories aloud to each other at various stages of composition.

Gender Roles

Unfair Game

Susan Jacoby

Questions for Study and Discussion (p. 209)

1. Jacoby's thesis is stated in paragraph 6: "In Holiday Inns and at the Plaza, on buses and airplanes, in tourist and first class, a woman is always thought to be looking for a man in addition to whatever else she may be doing." Her article demonstrates how untrue that stereotype is and was evidently written both to encourage women to assert themselves and to instruct men in common courtesy.

2. Jacoby advocates rebuffing the man with a polite but firm refusal and, should that fail, telling him "roughly and loudly" that his presence is a "nuisance" (17).

3. In paragraph 17 Jacoby explains, "Our mothers didn't teach us to tell a man to get lost; they told us to smile and hint that we'd be just delighted to spend time with the gentleman if we didn't have other commitments." Evidently she herself is not constrained by that code.

4. She manages to imply that had she not been in a hurry, she might have stayed over in Dallas with him--which is not true but which he will later have to explain to his wife.

5. Jacoby's essay is written in an assertive, straight-to-the-point manner. Her forthright "I do blame a man for trying in this situation" (15) and her crisp sentence fragments--"Simple courtesy. No insults and no hurt feelings" (19)--are examples of that tone.

Writing Topics (p. 210)

1. Women might be expected to have appreciated Jacoby's argument, and they did. The men, however, were less appreciative; many assumed that any woman without an escort in a bar or restaurant does intend to be picked up, or that the exceptions are so rare that such an assumption is natural and excusable. In preparation for writing their opinion letters, students may find it useful to read some letters to the editor in The New York Times (or the local newspaper) and discuss which are effective and which illogical or otherwise unpersuasive.

2. As always, it's the examples on which the effectiveness of the students' papers will depend. They might be encouraged to prepare for this

assignment by considering a wide range of situations--at home, in class, at work, with friends, or just on the bus--and imagining the likely effects of courtesy and discourtesy.

3. An interesting approach to this question is to have students compare articles on dating from a contemporary issue of a magazine such as Seventeen and an early-1980s issue of that magazine, using back issues or microfilm in the library. Your male and female students will likely have very different answers to the last part of the question--probably to their surprise.

"I'll Explain It to You": Lecturing and Listening

Deborah Tannen

Questions for Study and Discussion (p. 224)

1. In each of the four anecdotes, Tannen notes that the woman in each conversation was the audience and was never given the chance to participate equally in dialogue. The stories are effective as a beginning to the essay because they give concrete examples of what Tannen is trying to describe.

2. The study was pivotal to Tannen because it showed that even if a woman has expertise in a subject this does not ensure that she will be given the same treatment or credited with the same authority as a male expert. This idea was important to Tannen because her own experiences in conversation corroborated it and suggested there was more to study about male-female communication.

3. Tannen chooses to include Fox's findings because they support her thesis with empirical evidence. Fox's observations are more profound because they illustrate the fact that the tendency for men to lecture and women to listen begins at a young age and is not something seen only in adults. This pattern is troubling because it means that, though women are entering the work force with greater frequency and are becoming colleagues and even supervisors of men, difficulties in communication will persist.

4. Tannen has gathered information from other researchers' studies, anthropologists, personal situations, and the experiences of people she knows. Tannen's use of her own experiences as examples to support her research makes the information more real than if she only quoted other people's findings. She herself can offer firsthand testimony on the phenomenon. The two types of sources complement each other and make the essay richer and more varied.

5. Tannen tends to make a statement about men being overbearing, but almost immediately tries to lessen the impact of the statement by softening her stance or offering a mitigating circumstance. One example of this can be

found in paragraph 11 when she almost defends men who have the tendency to be overbearing in conversation: "Of course not all men respond in this way, but over the years I have encountered many men, and very few women, who do. It is not that speaking in this way is the male way of doing things, but that it is a male way."

6. Tannen writes that men tend to remember and tell more jokes than women because men use them to be the focal point of a conversation, whereas women do not remember or tell jokes as frequently because they do not wish to be the center of attention. Some students may find this to be true, others may not. Responses will vary according to both gender and personality type.

7. In paragraph 51, Tannen says, "When men begin to lecture other men, the listeners are experienced at trying to sidetrack the lecture, or to match it, or derail it. In this system, making authoritative pronouncements may be a way to begin an exchange of information." Tannen feels that women are unable to use this strategy because they are not accustomed to seizing the opportunity to speak; rather, they are accustomed to listening and waiting for a turn to speak.

8. Answers will vary for this question. Some students will have found the titles helpful, others may have considered them merely annoying. When taking into consideration which section titles they feel should be omitted, students should be prepared to say why. Female and male choices will probably differ.

9. Students may wish to discuss their present habits before discussing how they would change them. For example, the class may be full of women who tend not to let men dominate conversation or, on the other hand, there may be a majority of men who feel that they are open to talking on an equal level with both men and women.

Writing Topics (p. 225)

1. The suggestion to record a conversation for analysis will probably be helpful because students can hear themselves and also get feedback as to how other people perceive their conversational habits. Before writing the essay, students may wish to get comments from both sexes to see how the tape is interpreted by each.

2. Essays will probably conflict because women and men will tend to stick up for their respective gender. Men will probably not notice their faults and women will probably not see theirs; each will be quicker to attack the other gender. Students may wish to take specific types of conversations into consideration. For example, what differences or similarities are there between what men and women say to other men and women at funerals, parties, weddings, or business meetings? The last part of the assignment asks to take age into consideration. This is probably a discussion in itself, as

43

younger college students will most likely have interesting opinions about how their elders talk to one another and to those younger than them.

The Androgynous Man

Noel Perrin

Questions for Study and Discussion (p. 229)

1. In paragraph 7, Perrin states that "to be spiritually androgynous is a kind of freedom" that allows "a range of choices" not available, for example, to men who feel they have to imitate the stereotype of the "all-male, or he-man, or 100% red-blooded Americans."

Before revealing this definition Perrin felt it necessary to provide an example of how men are expected to fulfill certain roles and assume certain attitudes. This example serves as an effective introduction to the central issue of the essay--androgyny.

Perrin does not, however, use the strict dictionary definition of androgyny, which involves the physical combination of a man and a woman in one body. Instead, he clearly refers to a "spiritual androgyny" that incorporates the attitudes and behaviors of both stereotyped sexual roles into a lifestyle that offers a wider range of choices.

2. A thesis for this essay might read as follows: "Androgynous men and women live freer lives than those who struggle to fit themselves into stereotyped masculine and feminine roles."

Perrin's purpose is to convince readers not to feel obliged to live up to prescribed roles as a condition for their own self-esteem, especially since androgynes are spiritually freer and live richer lives than those who try to be what they feel is expected.

3. Perrin believes that androgynes have a wider range of choices in their lives and are therefore freer than those who feel compelled to imitate rigid gender stereotypes. To support this belief he provides a series of examples from his own experiences: being freed to serve as a nurturing father to his children; feeling free to kiss his cat; being unembarrassed about his ignorance of cars and household maintenance; and being more easily moved to public displays of emotion.

Students may find a couple of these examples less convincing than the others, and, after discussing with them which these might be, see if they can assess why Perrin has chosen the particular examples he has included.

4. Though the essay can certainly appeal to both sexes, especially since its central issue is androgyny, its focus on the qualities of the "he-man" and its selection of examples geared toward male behavior suggest that its primary audience is men.

5. The point of Perrin's last paragraph is that men should feel free to act unself-consciously, regardless of the types of behavior such freedom might elicit. The public display of emotion is effective in conveying this point because it is a classic example of the kind of behavior the stereotyped male would struggle to repress. Perrin suggests that <u>not</u> repressing such behavior is not a weakness but a kind of fulfillment.

Writing Topics (p. 229)

1. For a consideration of the pressure exerted on females to live up to certain sexual roles, students can review Susan Jacoby's "Unfair Game" (p. 207). After looking over her discussion of what is expected of women and men, and at Perrin's discussion of the "he-man," students may find it easier to identify how their own definitions of masculinity and femininity differ from prevailing stereotypes. Students may profit from a class discussion of how their own views of sexual roles differ from those of their parents.

2. Some students may find it helpful to approach this assignment from the opposite direction, recounting experiences where they were forced to recognize that formerly accepted stereotyped roles were, in fact, no longer valid. They can then discuss what effect this recognition has had on their views about other prescribed roles for men and women.

Rope

Katherine Anne Porter

Questions for Study and Discussion (p. 236)

1. A city couple is in the process of settling into the house where they will be staying for the summer. (They usually leave town for the summer-- see paragraphs 17 and 22--and certain details such as the need for curtain rods [20] and for fixing the sashes "this summer" [12] suggest that they own the house and have spent previous summers there.) They are disorganized partly because they have been there only two days (2) and have not yet made the transition from city apartment life (10) to the entirely different demands of living in a house several miles from the nearest village (24) and lacking the usual urban conveniences.

2. Both the man and the woman are plain-spoken and ordinary. They are quarreling about everything they can think of, but the cause of their disagreement is apparently the strain of having little money (4) and little time (22) for their summer vacation. The man offers to go back to town ostensibly to get his wife's coffee but also, perhaps, to escape from the quarrel--and perhaps his wife is not wrong in thinking he wants to avoid doing some of the housework (16).

3. From the wife's point of view, the story might provide an unflattering description of the husband but not of her and would elaborate upon her interior thoughts, feelings, suspicions, and frustrations, without having to take into account her husband's. But alert readers will have noted that though in the third person, "Rope" is told from the husband's perspective, as hinted at in paragraphs 9 to 10 and revealed in paragraphs 31 and 35.

4. Porter's use of indirect discourse distances readers from the quarrel. For some readers, it also adds a comic element to the story; one imagines a narrator reporting the quarrel like a boxing match, blow by blow, carefully converting pronouns and verb tenses but occasionally getting carried away: "But she was a little disappointed about the coffee, and oh, look, look, look at the eggs! Oh my, they're all running! . . . Hadn't he known eggs mustn't be squeezed" (6)? The use of loaded questions, a familiar tactic in knock-down-drag-out arguments, adds to this comic effect when they are reported with dogged literalness.

5. The tone of the couple's conversation modulates at several points. At first the wife is testy, the husband defensive (3-5); then she begins to scold and complain, while he tries to mollify her (6-9); he grows angry and she turns sarcastic (10-13); then he starts to criticize her and she gives as good as she gets (14-18); and finally, after more bickering, the wife breaks into sarcastic, then hysterical laughter and ends the argument by running from the room (29-30). These are, however, all variations of a single tone; the major shift comes at paragraph 32 when the couple has become conciliatory, tender, and above all calm. In effect the crescendo of anger up to paragraph 28 constitutes the rising action of the story; the wife's hysterical outburst (29-30) is the climax; and the conclusion (32-37) is the denouement in which the story's conflict has been resolved.

6. The whippoorwill, "clear out of the season" (36), sounds a romantic note at the end of the story. There's a hint, too, in paragraph 36, that the wife identifies the whippoorwill with her husband, who has also had problems with "his girl" but is "still coming back."

7. The rope is the ostensible cause of the couple's quarrel; the wife comes back to the subject again and again. But the rope also seems to represent the bond between the two characters, their marriage. This identification will not support a symbolic interpretation of the story. However, we assume the author chose a rope as the focus of the argument because of what rope does best: It ties things together.

Writing Topics (p. 236)

1. Here the responses of students who are married will differ from those of students with no personal experience of that intimate partnership. Married people do build up tensions and disagreements that an occasional argument can help to dispel--or make worse--according to the underlying

46

qualities of the relationship. Those who have been married may more readily acknowledge the benefits of clearing the air in this way, while those who have only observed other marriages, whether as children or as friends, are likely to take a darker view. A number of books for general readers take up various aspects of quarreling, among them Eric Berne's Games People Play, which interested students might be referred to.

2. One way for students to approach this assignment is to consider ways in which they might rationalize making an extravagant purchase or convince themselves that they really do need an item whose usefulness is questionable. Their analyses may reveal to them something about the nature of impulse buying and the motivation behind it.

<u>Men and Women in the Workplace</u>

The Importance of Work

Gloria Steinem

<u>Questions for Study and Discussion (p. 241)</u>

1. Students' responses should reflect Steinem's main concern--that women be allowed to work not just because they feel they have to, but because "productive, honored work [is] a natural part of ourselves and . . . one of life's basic pleasures" (22).

2. Many women greeted the <u>Wall Street Journal</u>'s definition of the working woman with cynicism because women have always worked, if not in the salaried labor force, in the "poorly rewarded, low-security, high-risk job of homemaking" (2). Steinem's response to the <u>Journal</u>'s definition is the following: "If all the productive work of human maintenance that women do in the home were valued at its replacement cost, the gross national product of the United States would go up by 26 percent" (2).

3. Steinem believes many women use this response to ward off criticism that they are not taking care of their children, or that they are unfeminine, or to confront men's resentment of them competing in the work force. The strongest objections Steinem has to this "Womenworkbecause-wehaveto" defense are that it ignores the rewards of work that women who use it are not confessing and that it can lead to considerable waste of human talents.

Steinem explains the significance of turning this phrase into a single word in paragraph 7: "The phrase has become one word, one key on the typewriter--an economic form of the socially 'feminine' stance of passivity and self-sacrifice. Under attack, we still tend to present ourselves as creatures of economic necessity and familial devotion. 'Women-

47

workbecausewehaveto' has become the easiest thing to say."

4. Steinem dismisses these claims by simply stating "that a decent job is a basic human right for everybody" (6).

5. Steinem applauds women who work even though they don't need to financially because they "are on the frontier of asserting this right for all women. . . . To prevent a woman whose husband or father is wealthy from earning her own living, and from gaining the self-confidence that comes with that ability, is to keep her needful of that unearned power and less willing to disperse it. Moreover, it is to lose forever her unique talents" (18).

6. In the Economic Recovery Act of 1946, "full employment" was reinterpreted and defined as "the employment of those who want to work, without regard to whether their employment is, by some definition, necessary" (13). Steinem strongly supports this definition and recognizes its importance, especially in bad economic times, since bad times often create a "resentment of employed women" (13).

7. According to Steinem, society benefits from full employment of men and women because it needs "all its members' talents" (12). Benefits to individuals are anchored by the notion that men and women both "are more satisfied with their lives" when they hold jobs by choice (11).

8. Steinem's article is firmly but calmly expressed and her main points well reasoned, making her an effective persuasive writer. She does not use a tone or diction that is openly hostile to women who may rely on the "Womenworkbecausewehaveto" defense, and thereby ingratiates herself with those readers who are most important to her purpose. Her explanations are logical and clearly reasoned, and the supporting information suited to the needs of her main idea.

9. This article seems intended mainly for women, particularly those who may rely on a "Womenworkbecausewehaveto" defense of their jobs. Steinem assumes that most of her readers will recognize that the points she raises about the value of holding a job are, for the most part, taken for granted with respect to men, and only come into question when they are applied to women. Her argument may therefore be more convincing for those who sympathize with that central premise than for those who would question the need for such an application in the first place, thereby obscuring their appreciation of her argument that women should openly recognize the value and rewards of the jobs they hold.

Writing Topics (p. 242)

1. A prewriting discussion for this topic may generate some lively debate on the issue of two-income families and society's obligation to protect the right of <u>both</u> parents to work. An analysis of this issue within the context of the position stated in the assignment may help students arrive

at some conclusions about the pros and cons of attempting to provide a job for <u>every</u> citizen.

2. Students may find it enlightening to share the results of this assignment and discover some of the effects that different parents' working situations have on their children's lives.

Summer Job

Mary Mebane

<u>Questions for Study and Discussion (p. 248)</u>

1. Mebane knew the work would be hard because several women in her neighborhood had already worked at American during the green season and had informed her that mostly whites worked on the "cigarette side" where the work was easy; she would, instead, work the belt on the "tobacco side" where it would be more difficult.

Had the section on the hiring process been shortened, Mebane's essay would be less effective. The monotony and aggravation the women endure while standing on line all day in oppressive heat, just to get jobs of such miserable circumstances, indicate how much they need the work and money these temporary jobs offer, and emphasize the discriminatory and exploitative practices of the tobacco company.

2. Mebane worked on two different belts once she was hired. On the first, she sifted through shredded tobacco and picked out pieces whose stems were too large. After only a short while there, she moved upstairs to "work up" bundles of tobacco onto another belt, making sure the tied ends faced her before the bundles went off to the cutter. At the end of her first day of such work, bending over barrels of tied tobacco leaves, then over the belt, and then back over the barrels, Mebane says she "found the work killing" (28).

3. So many women sought work at the tobacco factories because they could make "their chief money of the year" during the green season, as "the factory paid more money than days work" (1).

Since this work was temporary, though, it likely meant that most men could not afford to leave whatever permanent jobs they had, thereby making the work available to women instead.

4. Mebane uses contrast mainly to show the different conditions for African-Americans and whites. Before she even goes for the job, she realizes that the easy work on the cigarette side is mostly for whites and the "killing work" of the belts on the tobacco side for African-Americans. While waiting to be chosen for work, the mass of African-American women is left standing in the sweltering sun while the white men doing the hiring are in the relative comfort of the air-conditioned office. And when the pudgy man

49

occasionally appears to call the women to work, his manner is casual, indifferent, and nonchalant, in contrast to the pushing and shoving of the women as they struggle to be noticed and chosen for a job. This series of contrasts points up the injustice Mebane feels as she looks back on her experiences with the American Tobacco Company.

5. Mebane stayed on at her job only because her neighbors "were quite pleased that [she] had gotten on" and she did not "want to let them down" by quitting (28).

6. Students may cite instances of Mebane's use of detail from almost any section of the essay, but will probably focus most particularly on the two days she waits to be chosen and on each of the belts she works after she is hired. They should recognize that such detail helps convey a more accurate and concrete sense of what Mebane's experiences were like, making the underlying sense of racial injustice more strongly felt.

7. Mebane identifies the time, place, and circumstances of her narrative in the first two paragraphs. Her first sentence establishes the time as the summer of 1949. From there she explains the "green season" and that there were two tobacco companies in Durham, only one of which--American--hired temporary workers, thereby providing the place. In paragraph two, she reveals the rest of the circumstances needed to appreciate the beginning of the narrative proper, which begins with paragraph three.

Writing Topics (p. 249)

1. This topic provides a good opportunity to review elements of process analysis. Students will be concerned with "directional process" and can find a definition for that term in the glossary. In addition, you may wish to work through a model directional process essay with them, outlining the stages of a proposed essay according to how the steps in a selected process fall into place.

2. Since many students may not have any direct experience with full-time year-round employment, they may wish to approach this topic by considering how their attitude toward the summer jobs they've held was affected by knowing they would be finished working when the summer ended. How might they have felt if there were no such end in sight? By considering this idea, students may be better able to speculate on the differences and similarities that exist between summer and full-time work.

On Power

Barbara Lazear Ascher

1. In the first paragraph, Ascher defines legal power as synonymous with privilege, money, and respectability. It also translates into a lifestyle that includes travel, access to important people, and acquaintances in high social circles. Her definition would be similar for other professions that are high-paying, high-profile, and high-prestige in the United States, such as finance or medicine. It would probably be different if she had entered a profession such as teaching or social work. Her definition of power is not limited to male/female situations, as she says in paragraph 11. Her husband, a doctor, has also encountered this kind of power play in an upper-class hospital where his volunteer efforts were considered second-class.

2. When women achieve power, they forget their roots and their own struggles to get to the top. Ascher was distressed and disappointed to find that the female partner in her law firm did nothing to help other women climb the professional ladder. She says they do nothing to help because they do not want to "fall backwards" (8).

3. Ascher's experiences on her fourth-grade baseball team taught her how easy it is to fall into a pattern of not looking back. She learned that, once in power, she had to play a certain game and be aggressive in order to stay in power. The result was that she did nothing for her peers. In the fifth grade, she learned how easy it is to fall out of power and no longer be part of the "in crowd." When puberty hit, Ascher was suddenly "banished" from the team and relegated "to the powerless world of hopscotch" (25).

4. Ascher means that once someone is in power that person will do anything to stay in power. She notes in paragraphs 18 to 23 that this is essentially an immature way to live. With adults, such self-involvement is particularly upsetting because what is acceptable behavior for children is not for adults.

5. Power is alluring because it offers a sense of being on the inside or the fast track. The idea of power is complex because it is paradoxical. On the one hand, it promises a life of privilege; on the other hand, according to Ascher, it consigns a person to a life of paranoia and fear of losing status and once again become an outsider.

6. Ascher did not leave the legal profession because she did not have the talent or the intelligence. She was not forced out, but made a deliberate decision: She did not want to act the way she would have had to--with backbiting and self-interest--in order to become a law firm partner. She feared she would have had to deny her feminine side in order to rise in a male-dominated office and professional climate.

51

7. Ascher was not interested in the kind of power the legal profession offered. She obviously enjoys another kind of power, however, as a writer: that of influencing her readers through her books and articles.

<u>Writing Topics (p. 254)</u>

1. We like to have our students do a free-write on what power means to them. Next, we have them explore, either in writing or in open class discussion, situations in which they felt powerful or powerless and to determine why they felt that way.

2. In preparing to argue for or against the shortened work week, students would be encouraged to interview family members or friends who are in the work force. Especially helpful would be interviews with people who currently work flex-time. Making lists of the advantages and disadvantages of a shortened work week is essential both to planning and to writing convincing arguments.

Confessions of a Working Stiff

Patrick Fenton

<u>Questions for Study and Discussion (p. 260)</u>

1. Fenton feels that Seaboard World Airlines is insensitive to his needs as a human being.

He feels his job is very difficult and does not allow him to use his mind at all.

The immediate causes of his dissatisfaction are the "drudgery, boredom, and fatigue" (1) of his job.

Fenton continues to work for the airline because he wants to provide for his children and pay the mortgage. The job has dampened his enthusiasm and initiative, and he, therefore does not try to get another job.

2. The company, in our view, seems to be more interested in automation than in improving working conditions. The company's basic motive is profit, and it will improve working conditions if, and only if, profits are improved. There was apparently little likelihood of this occurring at Seaboard.

We feel that the airline company gets nervous about assertive employees because they appear to be stepping out of line--thinking is not regarded as part of the job.

3. The "leads," Fenton tells us, are "foremen who must keep the men moving" (16). Fenton feels that it is important to discuss them because they

are a prime example of employees who once had pride in their jobs but who now have only apathy.

4. Diction and imagery that suggest the regimented, prison-like existence of the men are found in paragraphs 11, 12, 15, and 16.

5. Paragraphs 5, 8, 18, and 30 rely heavily on concrete details. Incidents that dramatize the plight of the workers occur in paragraphs 13, 14, and 21 through 25.

In each case Fenton <u>shows</u> rather than <u>tells</u> us about the plight of the workers.

6. We feel that each of these similes is appropriate in its context. 7. Fenton means that he is a working corpse, that his job has taken the life out of him.

7. Fenton means that he is a working corpse, that his job has taken the life out of him.

8. According to Fenton, "It's not the hard work that breaks a man at the airline, it's the boredom of doing the same job over and over again" (19).

Writing Topics (p. 261)

1. Students may wish to focus on how the degree to which a job requires one to think is related to the satisfaction that can be derived from work. Students can also consider the traditional dichotomy of blue-collar versus white-collar employment, and evaluate the role that productive thought plays in our conception of each.

2. If students wish to do some research into the current state of relations between management and labor they can seek out any of the numerous recent publications that examine the role and quality of business in our lives. Two of the more prominent examples of such pop analyses are: <u>Megatrends: Ten New Directions Transforming Our Lives</u> by John Naisbitt; and <u>In Search of Excellence</u> by Thomas J. Peters and Robert H. Waterman, Jr.

3. Before undertaking this writing topic, students should endeavor to find out just what are the physical demands of each of these jobs. How has technology, for example, affected these jobs since the time Fenton wrote his article? Students may find it helpful to interview both men and women who hold jobs in the construction and warehousing fields. The results of such interviews will enliven their writing by making it up to date and real.

One Last Time

Gary Soto

<u>Questions for Study and Discussion (p. 269)</u>

1. Soto means that some of the people in the film reminded him of people he knew. Presumably, he is referring to poor people with ragged clothing who work hard at manual jobs for little pay. Seeing this type of person, either Indian or Mexican, is evocative for Soto and brings him back to a formative period of his youth.

2. Only when he began to work in the fields, especially at his mother's side cutting grapes, did Soto come to empathize with the physical pain she endured at her job. The constant stooping, rising, and cutting took a toll on Soto's ankles and back too. He was unable to appreciate her effort until he experienced the same thing: "I caught on," he writes in paragraph 2, "when I went to pick grapes rather than play in the rows."

3. The unending repetition of cutting grapes, filling his pan, and then dumping it into a long succession of trays among the rows of grapevines numbed Soto's body and mind. He was so bored he had to sing or daydream about baseball, the YMCA pool, and prospective girlfriends in order to keep going (10).

4. He was excited about the job, particularly because he looked forward to working like an adult. Soto planned to buy clothes for himself and a teapot for his mother. He was so eager to begin that he rushed to start cutting (3). By the end of the day he was tired, bored, and discouraged because his mother had gathered 120 trays of grapes compared to his 73.

5. The excitement and anticipation of the prospect of working in the fields was quickly replaced by sadness, even despair, because the work was so uneventful and tedious. The narrative of the first day lasts ten paragraphs to set the scene, but the next twelve days are exactly the same as the first--so much so that Soto does not even have to describe them. This impresses upon the reader the wearing nature of such boring and difficult labor. The job is actually doubly tiring: physically, because of all the bending and cutting, and emotionally (or intellectually), because it is so uninteresting.

6. Soto did not want to pick grapes anymore because the enjoyment he anticipated was quickly replaced by the harsh reality of the job. He felt that picking grapes was degrading and beneath him; he decided that he would "rather wear old clothes than stoop like a Mexican" (15). In order to stretch his wardrobe and make it appear more extensive than it actually was, he alternately wore new and old clothes to school on different days. For instance, he wore a new T-shirt the first day of school, an old one the next, and another new shirt the day after that. He writes that he was so creative

54

he "worked like a magician, blinding [his] classmates, who were all clothes conscious and small-time social climbers" (15).

7. Picking cotton was better because he was paid by the hour (21), instead of according to how much he cut, as with the grapes (5). Soto was not interested in school at this point in his life, so his career aspirations were limited. People told him frequently that he would not amount to much and that he would end up working in the fields, so that, he writes, "I began to believe that chopping cotton might be a lifetime job for me. If not chopping cotton, then I might get lucky and find myself in a car wash or restaurant or junkyard. But it was clear; I'd work, and work hard" (22). Because he was doing poorly in school, it looked as if this might end up being the case.

8. Soto returned to the vineyards with his family because he could not find any other work and, apparently, because he needed money badly enough that he would go back to a job he despised.

The very nature of migrant work makes laborers feel anxious, insecure, and powerless. Bad weather can easily wipe out crops, leaving nothing to pick; a physical ailment, even slight, can push a worker out of the labor pool, especially since a worker can easily be replaced. Above all, the monotony and low status of the work can damage a person's spirit and lead to a feeling that there will never be an alternative job or a way out of the social and economic situation.

<u>Writing Topics (p. 269)</u>

1. Responses will obviously vary. Students might be asked not only to identify realistically the type of work they will be doing in a decade, but also the career they would most like to have, as well as the one in which they would hate to see themselves. This exercise could be enhanced by asking them to envision a most or least likely personal situation, lifestyle, and place of residence.

2. Students will probably identify as chores the tasks they find most onerous, while sports or club activities will be seen as pleasurable "work." Where does schoolwork fit in? Ask them to rank all of their activities not only in terms of what is most or least pleasing but what is most or least profitable. They might expand this assignment to consider the work of their siblings and parents. Students who see an activity in a different way (for example, one might enjoy math homework while another despises it) could be paired to debate the issue and to persuade their peers of their position.

3. This straightforward analysis will yield more similarities than differences, but students should be encouraged to think about the contrasts: rural versus city work, for instance. Student responses will probably focus on how "no-brainer" jobs are deadening to the body, mind, and spirit. They should be asked to identify such jobs in their own communities and to consider the people who work in "anonymous" jobs, such as toll booth

collectors or supermarket cashiers. Students might also debate the pros and cons of white-collar and blue-collar jobs.

4. This essay would probably work best if anecdotal in form, which would allow students to practice writing a narrative meant to convey a central point. Gender bias might easily creep into the essays; perhaps male students could be required to think about women entering traditionally male professions and vice versa.

Teaching and Learning

Angels on a Pin

Alexander Calandra

Questions for Study and Discussion (p. 275)

1. Calandra appears to adopt (or at least does not contradict) the student's complain that American science and mathematics teachers do not teach the actual structure of their subjects but instead, "in a pedantic way," emphasize the nature and methods of scientific thought and the "deep inner logic" of the subject (13). An implicit, subsidiary point is that some teachers, such as Calandra's colleague, penalize students who think originally instead of parroting back the expected conventional answers (1).

2. The question was supposed to test the student's knowledge of the principles of physics, and specifically the relations between altitude and air pressure. It failed because the student, looking for an opportunity to make his point, noticed that nothing in the question referred to air pressure. A more precise question might have been: "Show how it is possible to determine the height of a tall building by measuring air pressure with the aid of a barometer."

3. The answer in paragraph 6 appeals most to the student probably because it is the most remote from physics--and the funniest. He avoided the conventional answer in order "to challenge the Sputnik-panicked classrooms of America" (13) and the stale methods of thinking taught there.

4. Calandra does not state why he did not give the student full credit. One may speculate that he was accommodating his colleague, who (from paragraph 1) was less open-minded than Calandra. Since even on the retest the question did not require the student to take air pressure into account, and since the student's answer reveals if anything a greater knowledge of physics than the conventional answer would have done, Calandra supplies no grounds for giving less than full credit. In effect, the "system" is "set up against the student" (1).

5. Calandra never tells us the conventional method for determining the height of the building. He also does not say what kind of teacher (or person) his colleague is, information that might have suggested a more specific motive for the student's rebellious conduct. The effect of these omissions is to focus attention on the student's ingenuity and on his complaint about American scientific education. 6. The essay's title, by referring to that famous scholastic debate, suggests that the exam question too may not only

have many possible answers but may also be a pointless question in the first place. (How often does one measure the height of buildings, and if at all, how often with a barometer, as opposed to surveying equipment, which would give a more accurate measurement?) The student's "scholasticism" consisted of pedantically taking the question word for word, regardless of its context in his physics course, in order to mock the pedantry of his instruction.

7. None of them requires a barometer to be used for the purpose it was made to serve; another object such as a ruler or a book would have served just as well. The answers are therefore all contrary in spirit.

Writing Topics (p. 275)

1. The question gives interested students a lead to a useful source: Edward de Bono, Lateral Thinking (and other books by him). Another source is James L. Adams, Conceptual Blockbusting. Lateral thinking involves finding new and unexpected uses for familiar objects (for example, using the jagged edge of a key to open packages) or new kinds of answers to an old problem (for example, disposing of garbage by converting it to methane gas). De Bono and Adams provide examples and exercises in lateral thinking, and their techniques have proven useful in scientific and corporate brainstorming.

2. This question inevitably involves the role of evaluation and grades in education, and students will have much to say on this topic. But tests can, of course, also be a teaching tool, giving students the opportunity to practice and apply what they are trying to learn. The last part of this question might be approached by setting up categories: examination questions that test students' memory of information, those that require the manipulation of data or the solving of problems, those that require students to think their way through to conclusions (as in essay examinations), and so on.

How I Learned to Read and Write

Frederick Douglass

Questions for Study and Discussion (p. 280)

1. The mistress's change, which involved going from helping Douglass to spurning him, is described in paragraphs 1 to 3. She went from being kindhearted to being as cruel as her husband. She stopped instructing Douglass and went out of her way to prevent his learning, as when she took newspapers away from him. This illustrates that bigotry drags down notonly the object of scorn through less than human treatment, but drags down the bigot as well, because the bigot acts on a base, inhuman level.

58

2. Douglass knew that reading and writing would be his ticket out of slavery and an impoverished life. On an immediate level, they would help him escape by enabling him to forge his own pass. In the long term, education would be the first step in his climb up the social ladder. Presumably, and this was borne out by history, he knew he would then be able to reach back and help those he left behind.

3. Master Hugh was right: Reading made Douglass yearn to be free. In paragraph 6, Douglass writes: "The more I read, the more I was led to abhor and detest my enslavers." Douglass felt trapped, betrayed, and repressed. He also grew angry as his wretched condition was made even clearer to him through his reading. But he kept going because he hoped to be free, as he describes in the first few lines of paragraph 7.

4. Douglass learned "the power of truth over the conscience of even a slaveholder" (6) as he read the dialogue in which a master and slave debate the merits of slavery. After the debate, the master voluntarily emancipates the slave. As a result of his reading, Douglass had the confidence "to utter [his] thoughts" on the evils of slavery.

5. It took Douglass about seven years to learn how to read and write. Most people probably would have given up long before that. His perseverance demonstrates many admirable qualities: patience, a tough spirit, single-mindedness.

As regards his character, Douglass was savvy enough not to be tricked by possible slave catchers (7); he was also clever and resourceful, tricking white boys into helping him learn: He traded bread for lessons (4) and got boys to teach him how to write by challenging them to a contest (8).

6. This selection is a reminiscence narrative in which Douglass shows anecdotally his progression from illiteracy to learning the letters of the alphabet to full reading and writing.

7. Obviously, this is the work of an educated man, but one who was educated by life as well as by books. Douglass learned the basics of reading and writing from books and combined them with the harder lessons of his life as a slave to make himself strong and determined. His use of language and the power of his example also indicate this type of street/school education. The fact that he wrote this memoir bears testimony to his success and admirable effort.

8. In the main, Douglass is measured, although he was never fully resigned to his fate as a slave and was angry at times, as in paragraph 6 when he confesses his hatred of slaveowners, and even temporarily discouraged. Still, he comes across as self-assured but not haughty (8).

9. In paragraph 1, he uses the phrase "mental darkness" to describe his state. In paragraph 2, "bread for the hungry . . ." indicates how selflessly his mistress originally acted. The "more valuable bread of knowledge" in paragraph 4 shows Douglass's appreciation of the life that education

promised him. When he refers to the "silver trump of freedom" in paragraph 6, he indicates the value he placed on escaping from slavery.

Writing Topics (p. 281)

1. Students should be encouraged to open up emotionally and discuss, perhaps, the death of a friend or family member, failure in school or sports, or some other important event. They should describe the event and then step back from it, as Douglass does, to reflect on its importance as they recall the event years after the fact. Adopting Douglass's structure of describing stages might help: the lesson, the story, the reflection. This should produce a unified essay that moves across time periods.

2. If the instructor leads the way, students might follow. Describe for the class your own experience of being turned on to reading as a child when you first read a book such as Treasure Island or the Little House series. Identify when you realized you were involving yourself in the story and when you shared that feeling with someone who had had a similar experience. With your example in mind, students should more easily be able to do this assignment.

Miss Duling

Eudora Welty

Questions for Study and Discussion (p. 285)

1. More than anything else, Miss Duling was a stern authority figure. She tolerated no disrespect or fooling around, was serious in everything she did, and sought order throughout her school. She set high academic standards and held to them rigidly. She looked serious and acted in a severe manner. In paragraphs 6 through 9, Welty illustrates her description of Miss Duling by employing anecdotes that capture her points. The governor's daughter, for instance, received no special treatment (8), and we learn that achievement in subjects was measured by Miss Duling's own stiff examinations (6). Welty seems to have had a healthy respect for Miss Duling, born more out of fear than love; she did not love the principal, Welty writes explicitly in paragraph 7, but instead feared her sharp face and demanding presence.

2. On the most basic level, the bell rang the time of daily exercises in the school. Miss Duling marked recesses, dismissals, and fire drills with it. It came to symbolize her authority and strict oversight of the school to the extent that it seemed to grow "directly out of her right arm, as wings grew out of an angel or a tail out of the devil" (6). She wielded the bell and her command of the school with gusto: "With a swing of her bell that took her

whole right arm and shoulder," Welty writes, Miss Duling's influence rang "militant and impartial" (9).

3. Welty's mother, like Miss Duling, wanted "unclouded perfection" (12); her father, meanwhile, was interested in his daughter's rising above the average student. He was, however, "much more tolerant of possible error" (13).

4. Miss Duling was clearly telling the legislators, most of them her former students, that she still held them to high standards, even though they were adults and no longer pupils in her school. In paragraph 5, she served them notice, in effect, that spelling still counted and, to keep them on their toes, went so far as to challenge them to a spelling bee with her students. Miss Duling was probably using the risk of embarrassment at losing to the students as incentive for the legislators to remain diligent.

5. Welty believes that one of the reasons for Miss Duling's authoritarian approach was to get the pupils in her school to take their studies seriously and enthusiastically. Even as a young girl, Welty tells the reader, she was eager to learn (7). Miss Duling's manner, therefore, was not necessary as a motivational tool for the schoolgirl Welty.

Writing Topics (p. 285)

1. Certain characters are charming, eccentric, even funny on paper. In person, however, they can be weird, frightening, or intimidating. The distance of the written word keeps the reader safe and separated from such characters, Welty seems to say.

Remembering "schoolteacher characters" can lead to a lively writing exercise; students should be encouraged to paint as clear a picture as possible of a favorite--or most feared--teacher. Ask them to focus on significant, illustrative anecdotes and details. Students should then be encouraged to add depth to these characterizations by trying to empathize with their teachers or turn their teachers' lives into fictional stories. Throughout, this assignment might be an opportunity to let students write about their own feelings on education, since school is such a central part of their lives.

2. This exercise will probably flow naturally from the previous one. Character descriptions could easily become strongly felt opinion pieces about how a certain teacher helped or hindered a student, at least from the student's perspective. Students might be asked to make the difficult distinction between the kind of person a teacher is and how successful and effective that teacher is when it comes to the subject matter of a particular course. Because the importance of experiences are common, students should be encouraged to share their writing, particularly if two students hold divergent opinions about the same teacher.

Theme for English B

Langston Hughes

<u>Questions for Study and Discussion (p. 288)</u>

   1. The instructor is saying, in effect, write about what you know. The result will then be "true"--that is, based on personal experience and conviction, therefore well grounded and sincere.

   2. The student has much in common with Hughes, as the headnote to the poem reveals, but there are differences: The student was born in Winston-Salem, North Carolina, and is twenty-two, while Hughes was born in Joplin, Missouri, and was nineteen when he attended Columbia. Once your students have discovered these distinctions, a productive discussion might follow on why Hughes chose to use such a speaker--or any speaker at all.

   3. First, Columbia University <u>is</u> on a hill and Harlem is not. But the reference has other significances: The university offers a way up and out of the poverty of the African-American ghetto; the university is also distanced from the lives of Harlem's African-Americans, as lines 34 to 35 and line 10 suggest, and doubtless most of those who teach and study at Columbia consider themselves socially as well as intellectually "above" Harlem.

   4. The student and instructor are part of each other in two respects: At the moment each is part of the other's life, and more generally each stands for an aspect of American life that shapes the society in which both live and therefore helps to define the character of each. In this sense, we are indeed all part of each other.

   5. The answer to this question depends mainly on what course we think "English B" is. We think it is freshman composition, or at least a prose-writing course, because in a poetry-writing course the instructor would not ask for "a page," and therefore a poem such as this one would not be what the instructor wanted. However, the poem does fulfill the specific requirements of the assignment, for it is about one page long and clearly "comes out of" the student.

<u>Writing Topics (p. 288)</u>

   1. Fundamentally this discussion turns upon the students' view of education as it is and as it should be. Teachers who learn from their students generally conceive of education as a process, a dialogue. The essays of Emerson, Calandra, Ward, and Scudder directly or indirectly describe teachers or styles of teaching. As a focus for the discussion, you may want to ask students to consider what if anything the teachers in each of those essays learn from their students.

2. Students generally enjoy this topic, with its implicit opportunity to criticize the writing assignments they have previously been given in this and other courses. However, they also discover that inventing stimulating and workable assignments is not as easy as they might have thought! In preparatory discussion you might invite the students to consider such factors as the purpose of their assignments, what kinds of results are desired and how they are to be judged, and the requirement that an assignment be intelligible to and manageable for a heterogeneous class such as their own. (The obvious follow-up to this topic is to ask students to write essays based on the assignments they think are the best.)

In the Region of Ice

Joyce Carol Oates

Questions for Study and Discussion (p. 303)

1. As a teacher, Sister Irene sees herself as "an instrument by which facts were communicated" (2); as a nun, "she saturated herself daily in the knowledge that she was involved in the mystery of Christianity," having "given herself happily to that life" (51). Her "vocation," in this context, does not mean her job, but rather her obligation to serve God and His purposes. (Many students may not be aware of this alternative definition of vocation, though it is in their dictionaries.) Strikingly, Sister Irene does not conceive of her dual roles as teacher and nun in relation to other people--at least not before Allen Weinstein compels her to.

2. In paragraph 36, Weinstein indicates to Sister Irene that he too is planning to teach. Later in paragraph 42, he expresses his passionate dedication to the humanities, which, as a teacher, he hopes to communicate to others: "So, I say that the humanist is committed to life in its totality and not just to his profession." But despite his commitment and his obvious intelligence, Weinstein shows no aptitude for dealing with others, especially those less gifted than himself, and that aptitude is of course a major requirement for being a successful teacher. He is, Oates notes in paragraph 31, "totally alone, encased by a miniature world of his own."

3. Part of the power of the story turns on the fact that Oates does not categorically say that Weinstein is insane. Without question he is troubled, eccentric, anguished, and unstable, his emotions are jagged and unpredictable, he is a "terrified prisoner" behind a "confident voice" (36), and he has apparently uncontrollable outbursts of rage. However, nothing he says or does in the story is clear evidence of insanity, and Sister Irene's interview with his father (who brought about Allen's hospitalization through personal influence--paragraph 75) does not answer the question either. Since most readers will have concluded one way or the other as they read,

the discovery that there is no conclusive evidence in the story should affect their reading of the story considerably.

4. Allen's father is his opposite: direct, unsubtle, decisive, and overbearing. It is also plain that they dislike each other intensely (see paragraph 77), and that dislike may be a cause not only of Allen's having been hospitalized but also of his volatile, eccentric character. Sister Irene's story is different (37), for her parents had been "whining, weak people, and out of their wet need for affection, the girl she had been . . . had emerged stronger than either of them, contemptuous of tears because she had seen so many." This helps to explain her impersonal attitude toward her work (see question 1 above), and perhaps also her handling of the final interview with Allen (82-108).

5. Weinstein is drawing human sympathy from Sister Irene, almost against her will (37), and therefore leading her toward obedience of Christ's commandment that we all love each other, even our enemies. Such feelings, which she has long suppressed and which take control of her as she grows more involved in Weinstein's plight (see paragraphs 50-52), come to a climax when she receives the letter from the sanatorium (55-59): "She understood now the secret, sweet wildness that Christ must have felt, giving himself for man, dying for the billions of men who would never know of him and never understand the sacrifice. For the first time she approached the realization of that great act" (59).

6. The issue here is partly the role of ideas in the world, partly how one defines reality. A literalist view, like Sister Irene's, would hold that only what a person can do, or perceive with the senses, is real, and that anything intangible (such as an idea) is less real, or unreal. But ideas are abstractions from experience and products of mental activity, and as such obviously have a direct bearing on people's actions and perceptions: They are real. One thinks of Freud's theory of the unconscious and Marx's of history and economics as examples of ideas that have changed the world by changing attitudes, behavior, and institutions.

7. See paragraph 56, the sixth line of Claudio's speech from Measure for Measure: "In thrilling region of thick-ribbed ice." The speech is about death, but the image of residing in a region of ice has specific reference to the story. Weinstein kills himself in Alaska, but the title more generally refers to the frozen state of Sister Irene's emotions, thawed only briefly by her encounter with Weinstein.

8. Sister Irene considers her identity as having been determined long since by a choice she has made--she doubtless thinks that the choice was in becoming a nun, though we may think it happened earlier (37). The last sentence, in which she acknowledges that she feels nothing at Weinstein's suffering and death, signifies her return to the "region of ice."

1. Roughly summarized, Sister Irene's is an ivory-tower view, with emphasis on scholarship and the imparting of knowledge, while Weinstein argues for the teacher's moral responsibility for students' lives as well as their minds and for the world outside the academy. The two views are not irreconcilable in principle, as Einstein's career suggests, but such reconciliation is not very common. The Nobel laureate Richard Feynman has observed that to do and teach physics well demands more time and concentration than most people have, and that consequently he has excluded much else from his life. And since the biologist Barry Commoner became a public figure and leader of the environmentalist movement in the late 1960s, he has published little of importance in pure biology. Students might consider the kind of temperament to which each view appeals and the likelihood that both can appeal to the same kind of person.

2. Students should try to convey what their schooling has been like rather than merely record their reactions to school. Comparing and discussing these papers in class should enlighten many students as to the variety of approaches and experiences their classmates have gone through.

3. Paul and Allen seem more similar (both are dreamers, romantics, and misunderstood) than different (Allen is more of an intellect). A central similarity is the fact that both feel stifled by school. Students might consider how schools inhibit or encourage creativity and a zest for learning, and whether that is the proper role of education at all.

Campus Issues of the 1990s

The Unromantic Generation

Bruce Weber

Questions for Study and Discussion (p. 314)

1. Weber wanted to find out if recent college graduates are as cynical and materialistic as they are imagined to be by the rest of society. He expected to find among young adults traits similar to those his generation exhibited when they were in their twenties. As he says in paragraph 12, he felt he would be "plumbing a little of [his] past." Instead, Weber found logical and practical planners.

2. Weber is admiring of the new young generation as evidenced in words and phrases such as "news-conscious," "media-smart," "sophisticated," "distinct," "planners," "they have priorities," "they are not

heartless, soulless, cold, or unimaginative." Weber does make reference to them being "self-preoccupied," but defends them by saying all "youthful generations have always been," and that this generation is finally aware of it.

3. Weber defines his survey group in paragraph 8 as "between the ages of twenty-two and twenty-six. . . . , graduated from college, are living in or around an urban center, and are heterosexual . . . . They are planners." These people differ in their views about marriage, but basically agree that it is inevitable. This group is not representative of today's youth on the whole, excluding as it does the working class, those who marry right out of high school and pursue an education later, and those who go to college, fall in love, and then quit school. For the group it represents, this study does seem to represent accurately the goals and determination of today's graduate.

4. Young people look for monogamy, practicality, and a relationship that will not threaten their financial stability or career.

5. Weber explains that the threat of AIDS has led to diminishing sexual promiscuity. "Forecasts of economic doom," housing problems, and the "chaotic" future make young people want to establish themselves professionally before marriage and maintain their careers afterwards.

6. Weber implies that because of the changing world, the younger generation is acting in a way essential to their financial stability and health. They fear that promiscuity will lead to AIDS or other sexually transmitted diseases. Illogical, impractical career choices may lead to undesirable financial situations. However, practical thinking may be boring and the high standards it demands may lead to burnout.

7. Weber defines young people's view of romance as "inevitable" and "restricting." However, first he presents sufficient examples, quotations, and theories to support this statement, so that when he finally utters it, it rings true.

8. When Weber speaks of AIDS as the factor that will bring romance back to the younger generation, he points to the chilling thought that the specter of death and not more benevolent forces might inspire romance.

Writing Topics (p. 315)

1. Before beginning this essay, it may be beneficial for students to review the basics of organization so they can group the information they collect in a manner effective for their argument.

2. Students will find research materials in the library under the subject headings Love and Marriage. Of the recent books alluded to in the assignment, we suggest in particular those by Ernest Van Den Haag, beginning with The Invention That Isn't Working.

Sexual Correctness: Has it Gone Too Far?

Sarah Crichton

<u>Questions for Study and Discussion (p. 323)</u>

1. One camp promotes a cult of victimization that, according to Crichton, encourages fear, suspicion, and a defensive attitude on the part of women toward men. The opposing camp reacts against these ideas, saying that this cult of victimization hurts women because it implies that women are less independent than men and in need of protection from them. In addition, the opposing camp charges that such an attitude continues to make women junior partners in business and personal relationships.

2. Katie Roiphe, introduced in paragraph 17, is the author of a controversial book, <u>The Morning After: Sex, Fear and Feminism on Campus</u>. Roiphe says that women have become weak, easily offended, and touchy about sexual issues. Feminists, Roiphe contends, are ironically hurting themselves.

3. By "cloudy waters," Crichton refers to sexual situations in which consent is ambiguous. The so-called Antioch rules have come under much criticism, but they do attack this issue had on by requiring both parties to state explicitly their intentions and desires. Legislation of sexual behavior from above is unlikely to be popular with students, who will probably emphasize free and honest discussion between partners.

4. At Antioch College, partners must request verbal permission to proceed in a sexual act every step of the say (2). Crichton thinks the policy goes too far and that it destroys the magic of sexual discovery (3). In addition, she thinks the policy promotes the notion that men, not women, are in charge of a sexual situation (4).

5. Crichton calls Roiphe's book "loosely documented" (19). An example is Roiphe's refutation of the claim that one of every four women is raped at some point in her life. Roiphe claims to know that the statistic is overblown merely on the basis of her own circle of acquaintances. In response, applying Roiphe's anecdotal method herself, Kathy Pollitt examined her own acquaintances' experiences and emerged with a tally of abuse that suggests the one-in-four statistic might be, if anything, understated. Pollitt's point is that anecdotal evidence is no substitute for objective data. Crichton more or less agrees, yet seems to dismiss both sides of this argument by taking a glib pot shot at Pollitt: "It's punch-my-victim-card time: How full's yours?" (22).

6. Crichton thinks too much is being made of these complaints. She is even contemptuous of some of them, as indicated by her comments: "Oh, please," "So tell him to bug off," and "Tell them to get some therapy and cut

it out" (26). Simple incidents, she seems to say, do not make a major issue. She is certainly not sympathetic to many claims of harassment.

7. Crichton wants dialogue, not animosity, between the sexes on college campuses (32). Animosity builds suspicion, not trust. Such suspicion, Crichton fears, will spill over into child rearing; wary young women and defensive young men may grow up to impart gender stereotypes to their children. As she says in paragraph 33, rules do not impart the knowledge and flexibility that help people make informed decisions. She thinks that in college students should learn how to think and choose wisely in many situations, including sexual ones.

8. Her use of contractions and questions throughout gives the essay a chatty tone. It appears that the author intends to be conversational, not doctrinaire; she wants to talk common sense and admits that gray areas often exist in the matters she is considering. Some of her colloquial expressions include: "Back in the dark ages" (6) and "As a what?" (16). Her voice and tone are effective except when they also indicate disdain, as, for example, in paragraph 26. Many students may feel her tone is too casual for the matters she is discussing.

Writing Topics (p. 324)

1. Women especially may react to this writing topic with vehemence. Students of both genders should be asked to consider Crichton's two sides of feminist politics and to suggest others. Then they might take a stand based on one of them. They should be encouraged to move from polemics to persuasive argumentation. Students (the male ones, perhaps) should react and discuss where they stand on this issue. How do they feel, for instance, about always being seen as the aggressor and therefore a proper target for automatic suspicion from women?

2. This exercise might focus on rules: Are dos and don'ts effective for the students? Did they learn by doing or be being told what to do (or not to do) by their parents and teachers? What kind of job do they think their parents are doing? How might they change this? Do they see differences in the way boys and girls are raised: Are they forced into gender roles? Students might compare how child rearing is similar and different in large and small families, in families of various ethnic groups and religions, in families with children all of one or the other gender, and in families with both boys and girls.

3. If this assignment is too long given the circumstances of the course, perhaps students can read the introduction or first chapters of Roiphe's book and then compare it with Pollitt's New Yorker essay mentioned by Crichton. Mechanics and structure can be explored along with content; students might compare the authors' use of evidence and argument to evaluate their respective cases.

College Is a Waste of Time and Money

Caroline Bird

Questions for Study and Discussion (p. 333)

1. Bird summarizes her reasons for believing college to be a waste of time and money in paragraphs 53 to 56: (1) college doesn't make people intelligent, ambitious, happy, or liberal; (2) college can't claim much credit for the learning experiences that really change students; (3) even motivated students are disappointed with their college courses and professors; and (4) a college diploma no longer opens as many vocational doors.
   Students' responses to these reasons may vary.
2. In her first paragraph Bird states that the majority of college students are in school "because it has become the thing to do or because college is a pleasant place to be; because it's the only way they can get parents or taxpayers to support them without working at a job they don't like; because Mother wanted them to go, or some other reason entirely irrelevant to the course of studies for which college is supposedly organized."
   Students' reactions to Bird's assessment may vary, and discussion of this question in class can yield some lively debate.
3. Bird believes students now protest "individually rather than in concert," by turning inward and withdrawing from active participation. As a result, those who feel discontent often opt to drop out and travel, or "refuse to go to college at all. . . . [Or] simply hang around college unhappily and reluctantly" (8). Students' opinions on whether this is accurate for their campus may vary, though most will probably recognize particular cases where Bird's assessment is applicable.
4. According to Bird, "students are sad because they are not needed." The work force is already overcrowded and "there is no room for so many newly minted 18-year-olds" (12).
   Students' responses to this evaluation may vary. Some may take issue with the central premise that students are, in fact, sad.
5. Bird recognizes "there is a certain unreality to the game" because she knows that parents do not hand over the money for college in one lump sum, and because she understands that financial considerations are rarely the <u>sole</u> criteria for sending children to college. As she states in paragraph 29, "Quite aside from the noneconomic benefits of college, and these should loom larger once the dollars are cleared away, there are grave difficulties in assigning a dollar value to college at all."
   Students' responses to Bird's belief that "few parents are sophisticated enough to understand that . . . their children would be better off with the money than with the education" may vary. This is another question that can serve as the focus for lively debate in class.

6. Bird quotes an economic dictionary to explain that psychic income is "income that is reckoned in terms of pleasure, satisfaction or general feelings of euphoria" (37). More generally, it is simply the "nonmonetary rewards of work" (37). People can estimate the value of psychic income by measuring the importance they attach to being happy and content in the work they do, regardless of the amount of money they make.

Students will no doubt recognize the value of psychic income for all individuals, but the degree to which they ascribe it importance may vary.

7. The "new vocationalism" Bird refers to is the recognition on behalf of college administrators and professors that one of the basic purposes of education is career preparation, and so they've begun to place an emphasis on the "ethic of achievement and service" in addition to the more traditional idealistic goals of higher education. Students will probably agree that this attitude remains a campus reality in the 1990s.

8. Bird uses a wide range of sources to substantiate her argument. In addition to the general description, in paragraph 11, of how she went about her research, she cites the following specific sources to lend credibility to the individual points she raises: (1) economist Fritz Machlup; (2) educator Nevitt Sanford; (3) the Carnegie Commission; (4) Richard Baloga, a policeman's son; (5) Sol Linowitz, once chairman of a committee of the American Council on Education; (6) author Daniel Yankelovich; (7) Leon Lefkowitz, social studies chairman at Central High School in Valley Stream, New York; (8) a sociologist; (9) Stephen G. Necel, a young banker in Poughkeepsie, New York; (10) Christopher Jancks, author of Inequality; (11) Jacob Mincer of the National Bureau of Economic Research and Columbia University; (12) the Department of Labor; (13) Jerry Darring, an Indianapolis man who returned to school after working a number of years; (14) thirty Vassar psychology majors; (15) John Shingleton, director of placement at Michigan State University; (16) the American Enterprise Institute; (17) Charles Lawrence, producer of a Chicago television show; and (18) Glenn Bassett, a personnel specialist at G.E.

The sheer number and variety of sources represented here, together with the information elicited from the, argue against Bird being merely opinionated, cynical, or sensational.

9. Paragraphs 52 through 57 summarize the issues Bird has elaborated upon in her essay. They are an effective conclusion because they organize the points in almost list fashion, helping readers put them into a comprehensive and coherent perspective when finishing the essay. This is not possible in the body of the essay because of the discussion and explanation that accompany each point.

Writing Topics (p. 334)

1. As a prewriting activity for this topic you can discuss with students

what their acquaintances from high school who did not go to college are currently doing. As part of your discussion, have students examine how valuable the examples presented might be as "possible learning experiences and opportunities for personal growth." This may help students formulate their opinions about the range of alternative learning experiences available to them.

2. It may be worthwhile to share the results of this assignment with students, particularly if they have sensed an overemphasis on financial concerns in Bird's analysis of the value of a college education.

The Recoloring of Campus Life

Shelby Steele

Questions for Study and Discussion (p. 347)

1. As Steele says in paragraphs 3 and 4, racial tension on campus should not be expected from a generation raised in the Great Society. Current college students grew up in a time of increasing racial equality and integration, at least in theory. The incongruence Steele sees stems also from the fact that campuses used to be safe havens, isolated from the harsher realities of the outside world of business and social difficulties. In the 1960s, in fact, Steele recalls that campuses were "oases of calm and understanding in a racially tense society" (3). He remembers no major clashes between black and white students and no white protests against blacks attending classes.

2. Steele left the campus where he taught, where racial tension was not very strong, and traveled to other California campuses where there had been black-white conflict. This method of investigation is valuable because it is experiential and subjective. A detached, statistical version of the "truth" would probably distort reality, because it would be based not so much on flesh-and-blood reactions, but on perceptions and intended responses.

3. Racial tension on today's college campuses seems to be about "white racism and black protest," but it is really--and ironically--"the result more of racial equality than inequality" (6).

4. The "politics of difference" is the affirmation of uniqueness that promotes separatism instead of unity, as indicated in paragraphs 8 to 9. It emerged from affirmative action programs, according to Steele, and other steps taken to redress past wrongs. Groups today often focus on what makes them different from other groups, instead of recognizing what the groups share on a level more fundamental than skin color or ethnic origin, which are qualities that students most readily grab on to when trying to define themselves by laying claim to their personal identities.

71

When difference equals power, proclaiming differences leads to getting and using power; this is almost always accomplished at another group's expense.

5. This myth assumes that blacks are inferior to whites in every way: socially, genetically, intellectually. It is a myth that has long been ingrained culturally and legally, so ingrained that it is hard to avoid on college campuses. This myth is even harder to avoid on campus because it is joined with the natural fears and anxieties of all students starting college; those fears are exacerbated among blacks by a fear that the myth of inferiority might be true. Steele seems concerned that racist overtones of inferiority and superiority taint all encounters on campus and can ignite tensions waiting for a spark.

6. Using race as a source for entitlement or special treatment enforces the historical privileges that Steele is fighting (29). He does not want blacks to feel that their race is "an extra right in itself" (25), as it was, de facto, for whites.

7. Exaltation of difference leads to separation and contrast instead of to community, according to Steele. People define themselves by pointing to the historical experience of their ethnic group, making such collective experiences absolutes that must not only be recognized but also revered. Steele is not necessarily against all differences, but he does oppose the movement that makes difference the ultimate measure of social importance and value.

8. Guilt is the essence of white anxiety; guilt additionally entails the terror that the guilt might in fact be justified. The darkest fear of whites is discovering that whites consider themselves superior because they made blacks feel inferior. Coupled with black anxiety that the myth of their inferiority might be true, this fear leads to "a suspicion of incomplete humanity" on the part of both blacks and whites (34).

9. Anxiety and integration are mixed because whites do not push for integration, since they perceive blacks do not want it. This leads to "voluntary segregation," according to Steele: "To avoid the anxieties of integrated situations, blacks ask for theme houses; to avoid guilt, white administrators give them theme houses" (39). To reduce racial tension on campus, Steele suggests a change in attitude: Students should understand their commonality and not dwell on their diversity. There will be no resolution to racial tension if the politics of difference results in further exclusivity and competition, instead of Steele's goal of respect for uniqueness and commonality. A sense of difference, he argues, can actually help black and white students realize that what they share is greater than what separates them. An appreciation of this should foster the idea that common ground transcends and outweighs any racial differences that exist.

10. Black students need better academic achievement and lower dropout rates, according to Steele. They must improve their own situations

and gain academic parity with whites. Colleges can help black students achieve these goals through challenge and encouragement, not through favored treatment or easy rides. He wants to see university administrators dismantle "the machinery of separatism, breaking the link between difference and power, and skewing the formula for entitlement away from race and gender and back to constitutional rights" (42).

Writing Topics (p. 347)

1. In order to encourage the communication Steele would like to see fostered among college students of different races, black students can interview white students and vice versa in an attempt to get them to see the other side of issues on a personal level. After describing the current state of affairs in their essays, students might reflect on what the future could be and how it could come about in their own school.

2. Students might discuss whether Steele is fair to black and white students or whether he is basing his opinions on stereotypes or a skewed sampling of college campuses, since he visited only California schools for this essay. Do black students think he is unnecessarily chastising them? Do white students think he has misrepresented them?

Let's Tell the Story of All America's Cultures

Ji-Yeon Mary Yuhfill

Questions for Study and Discussion (p. 350)

1. Yuhfill's thesis is that many immigrant ethnic groups contributed to the formation of American culture and society, yet the story of this collaboration is incorrectly told because the efforts of white people are disproportionately stressed at the expense of almost every other group. Yuhfill wants to correct the story by broadening the picture presented in history courses.

2. Yuhfill felt she was not getting the whole, true story of how American society was formed. She was hearing only one side of the story of Manifest Destiny, for instance, because the situation of Native Americans was misrepresented. The history she learned was one-sided and focused almost exclusively on an optimistic, unchallenged portrait of white progress. She did not learn about minority groups of other races and ethnic origins; presumably, as well, her history text focused on men much more than women.

3. For Yuhfill, the New York State report was important because, for the first time, she heard educators express the same concerns she had. Yuhfill realized, in effect, that she was not alone in her perception, and she saw the

report as the first step in correcting the important gap in education so that future students would not be hampered by a misleadingly narrow portrayal of American history.

4. Multiculturalists want the whole story of the United States told in history and social studies textbooks and curricula through the inclusion of many different perspectives on major events in American history. The multiculturalists want to stress the diversity--the "e pluribus"--of the American population and American history. Their opponents fear that this will put ethnic minorities, however small, on an equal footing with every other group and, ironically, also give an incorrect impression of how the United States developed as a nation. These opponents want to stress the unity--the "unum"--of the American population. Each side presumes its position to be correct; there has been little common ground in the recent debate on this topic.

5. Yuhfill's tone is exhortatory. She laments the gaps in her own education that made her feel like an outsider, but instead of bemoaning her past, she takes the New York State report as a sign of an optimistic future. Yuhfill issues a clarion call for change. This is most evident in some of her straightforward one-sentence paragraphs: "Well, the history books were wrong" (9) and "America changed them, but they changed America too" (11). She exhorts the reader to follow her ideas in paragraphs 17 and 22.

Writing Topics (p. 350)

1. Students might write both a preamble and a curriculum or syllabus. They can make an argument to support inclusion of every event, person, or primary source. They might also write a dialogue between an advocate and an opponent for multiculturalism. Students will probably feel strongly about this issue; differences in race, gender, and ethnic background could lead to vocal opinions that can be channeled into a persuasive written argument.

2. Students from different backgrounds will respond to this topic in diverse or maybe even contradictory ways. They should be encouraged to include their own experiences, but not to let emotions carry their arguments. This assignment can be turned into an attempt to reflect objectively on subjective circumstances to make a claim that is personal and substantial.

Language, Prejudice, and Sexism

The Language of Prejudice

Gordon Allport

Questions for Study and Discussion (p. 362)

1. Allport states his main idea most directly in paragraph 3: "The very act of classifying forces us to overlook all other features, many of which might offer a sounder basis than the rubric we select." Allport's supporting argument may be summarized as follows: First, he demonstrates the effect of certain commonly used, apparently innocently descriptive words that actually function as "symbols of primary potency" (blind, Chinese, Jew) and block out our awareness of a person's other characteristics. Allport then examines the negative connotations that categorizing words often carry, whether deliberately or through their cultural associations. As a case in point, he traces the use of the label "communist" in America after World War I, showing that it functioned as a "verbal symbol" to discredit a certain element of society. Finally, through two historical examples, Allport shows that mere words can arouse as powerful a reaction as their referents.

2. Though nouns are essential tools in "clustering" our perceptions, Allport notes that "each label we use, especially those of primary potency, distracts our attention from concrete reality" (6) and "magnifies one attribute out of all proportion to its true significance, and masks other important attributes of the individual" (6).

3. Labels of primary potency, says Allport, "act like shrieking sirens, deafening us to all find discriminations that we might otherwise perceive" (4); that is, they are particularly capable of causing us to view a person as a stereotype rather than as a complex individual with a host of different attributes. Though such labels may sometimes be unavoidable, their force can be greatly diminished by changing them from nouns into adjectives (9).

4. Depending on the part of the country students are from, some may be surprised or amused at some of Allport's examples. For example, where anti-Catholic prejudice is unknown the term papist will hardly have much emotional impact. On the other hand, seeing words such as nigger, wop, and kike in print (11) always has shock value, and emphasizes Allport's point about the qualitative difference between such words and the more neutral Negro, Italian, and Jew. (Since Allport wrote, of course, African-American and black have largely displaced Negro, and Asians are rarely called "yellow.") The last part of this question invites students to consider that

such words exist for the sole purpose of expressing prejudice; when prejudice recedes, the words fall out of use.

5. Though the label <u>communist</u> is no longer used as frequently as it was in the 1950s to designate a scapegoat in American society, it is still commonly employed to designate a perceived threat in the rest of the world. Thus, rebels in Southeast Asia, Central America, and Africa are often termed "communist" rather than "nationalist," though their politics have little or nothing in common.

6. When an individual emphatically rejects designation by a particular label on the basis of the word's associations rather than its accuracy, he or she is displaying symbol phobia (32). In paragraph 34 Allport explains verbal realism: "When symbols provoke strong emotions they are sometimes regarded no longer as symbols, but as actual things." Thus, many women who espouse complete equality for their sex will refuse to be called "feminists" or "women's liberationists," and those who argue about whether abortion should be legal prefer to be labeled "pro-choice" and "pro-life" rather than "pro-abortion" and "anti-abortion."

<u>Writing Topics (p. 362)</u>

1. This exploration begins as an exercise in classification: The students are to define themselves in terms of general attributes they share with some people but not with others. Beyond this, the question asks them to consider the relation between the way they see themselves and what they believe strangers (responding to what Allport calls "labels of primary potency") would think of them. Finally, the students are asked to consider how Allport's "emotionally toned labels" have impinged on their lives. African-American, Jewish, and other minority students will doubtless have stories to tell, but so may others: the studious one who was called a grind or an egghead, for example.

2. This question calls for some library research. Since the issue of labels almost inevitably involves prejudice, students should begin their search with sources classified under the subject heading Prejudices and Antipathies (this is where Allport's <u>The Nature of Prejudice</u> is catalogued) and possibly move from there to more specialized subject headings: Feminism, for example, if they are doing research on women, or Negroes--Race Identity (through 1976) and Blacks--Race Identity (since 1976--this change itself is an example of the phenomenon) for African-Americans.

The Meanings of a Word

Gloria Naylor

Questions for Study and Discussion (p. 366)

1. As Naylor explains in paragraph 2, words acquire meanings through their usage and the context of that usage. A word, in this case nigger, means one thing when spoken by black people to black people but another when spoken by white people to black people.

2. In paragraph 1, she explains that the written word can never capture the force, flavor, and life of the spoken word. "Context" is the place, time, and situation in which an act takes place, in this case the use of the word nigger.

3. The contradiction is that, in the author's home, nigger was not a word spat out as an invective or insult; it was not meant to harm. She chronicles this usage, which was a common part of her daily life, throughout the rest of the essay. At school, however, the word was used for a different purpose: to curse her. When she remarked that she had once again received a higher score on a math test than a boy in her class, he responded by calling her "nigger."

4. "Nigger," in the family's context, meant someone who stood out for having done something honorable and noteworthy, such as work hard to save money for a mortgage (8) or stand up with pride to someone such as a foreman (9). On the other hand, when used by her family in the plural, "niggers" were people who acted dishonorably, such as failing to care for their children or find employment (10). She offers little explanation of her classmate's use of the word because she feels that his meaning is clear to the audience. As readers, students might feel accused: They know what it means! Others, however, will immediately empathize.

5. Naylor vividly describes in lively detail the bustle of the weekends by showing who dropped by and painting a picture of them relaxing. She also uses words with punch to illustrate the activity: Conversations were "punctuated by the sound of a baby's crying," "it was a bustling and open house," people were always "popping in and out to exchange bits of gossip." Because of the jovial, comfortable atmosphere, the word nigger was used with familiarity, not disdain.

6. "Girl" was a mark of respect when used to indicate a woman's toughness and grit: "the extra ounce of wit, nerve, or daring that the woman had shown" (11). Most women find the word demeaning; it is often used to put women down or treat them as children or as second-rate compared to men. In professional situations, in particular, the word can be condescending and disrespectful.

7. Naylor's tone is moderate, measured, and persuasive. She does not

set out to preach or rant, but to explain. In paragraph 2, the author says that she is "not going to enter the debate." Recounting the story of the boy's use of "nigger," she does not rail against him, but relates the incident almost dispassionately. She remarks simply, "I don't agree," in paragraph 14 and ends the essay with the quiet moment when her mother explains the word to her. This reserve actually gives the essay power because Naylor has shown that it is a reasoned, not an emotional response.

8. Naylor means that her mother knew her daughter would someday learn a painful lesson and that, having heard the word nigger used derisively, the time had come to explain gently what had happened. The last sentence nicely buttons up the piece; the light touch ironically leaves the reader with a deep impression.

9. Her family's use of the word nigger as praise in paragraphs 6 to 9 supports her assertion that, in a black context, the word denoted praise. In paragraph 10, though, the use of the plural shows a certain disdain, although not a racist disdain. As she explains in paragraph 14, her family used the word in human, not racial terms. It can be argued, however, that the black community took from the white community the negative aspect of the word when applying it to a black person who was not worthy of praise.

Writing Topics (p. 367)

1. The issue of self-definition is an important one. The psychiatrist Thomas Szasz says that "The struggle for definition is veritably the struggle for life itself. . . . He who first seizes the word imposes reality on the other: he who defines thus dominates and lives; and he who is defined is subjugated and may be killed." Before starting on this topic, students should be encouraged to reread Gordon Allport's essay, "The Language of Prejudice," in particular, those sections in which he discusses the power of labels.

2. Ask students to list what they think of when they hear the words before looking them up. As part of this exercise, they might consider the points made by Alleen Pace Nilsen in her essay "Sexism in English: A 1990s Update" (p. 377). Students should also think about how the meanings of the words have changed, particularly in recent years, as people have become more sensitive to gender-specific language. They might discuss whether people are too touchy and whether, if we removed all descriptive slang words, language would be colorless and neutral. Would such removal mark the progress or decline of language?

Defining the "American Indian": A Case Study in the Language of Suppression

Haig Bosmajian

Questions for Study and Discussion (p. 375)

1. Language can be used to justify reprehensible acts. In fact, sloppy language can even lead to irresponsible deeds. If words have no solid meaning, they can be twisted at will and any action can be made to at least sound proper. Words and deeds are therefore in a symbiotic relationship; it is important to keep in mind that one affects the other directly and with great consequence.

2. Natural-religious redefinition is discussed in paragraph 5. Indians who resisted invasion of their lands were considered heathens by the Puritans, and once so labeled, Puritans could justify their annihilation. Those Indians who converted were seen as noble savages who had an innate goodness that the white man brought forth. However, the conversion aspect of the Puritan mission was closely allied (albeit in a secondary role) to territorial goals.

3. The Indians were made "governmental nonentities" through a series of legal precedents. In 1787, the Constitutional Convention defined each black slave as three-fifths of a person, but counted Indians as nothing (8). Because Indians had no legal standing, they had no legal rights to property or even to their own lives to which they could appeal in court. Even the right to ask for justice from a court was denied to them. The Minnesota Supreme Court ruled in 1897 that "Indians as a race are not as highly civilized as whites" (11); Minnesota also said that Indians could not vote because they were not civilized (12). Arizona lumped Indians together with traitors and the insane, saying they could not manage their own affairs (13).

4. By the time Indians received the right to vote in Arizona (1948), they had lost much of their property and had to struggle to maintain their heritage. Their ability to participate in government was hampered by their poor economic situation, as well as by a long-held stereotyped image of Indians as lazy, untrustworthy outcasts.

Writing Topics (p. 376)

1. Library research should be employed in this exercise. If students live near an Indian reservation or community, they should try to contact local Indian leaders to get their side of the story of regional history. In this way, this exercise can be made relevant to the students' experiences and locale. Ask them also to list the words or phrases that come to mind when

79

discussing Indians (as in paragraph 10) to consider if negative connotations can be applied to the local Indian experience.

2. Nazi Germany's use of propaganda to dehumanize the Jews can turn this writing topic into a primary or secondary source assignment with connections to history. Using Bosmajian's sources (footnote 1), students can see how the Nazis progressively built up a linguistic atmosphere against the Jews. They might also consider examples from movies such as <u>Swing Kids</u> and <u>Schindler's List</u>. Students might also think about how the use of racial or ethnic slurs in their own school turns fellow students into outsiders instead of individuals. Finally, students should consider one or more of the following groups: ethnic factions in the former Yugoslavia; various African tribes involved in civil unrest; Arabs and Israelis; ethnic groups in the former Soviet Union, Catholics and Protestants in Northern Ireland, and gays and lesbians in America.

Sexism in English: A 1990s Update

Alleen Pace Nilsen

<u>Questions for Study and Discussion (p. 387)</u>

1. Nilsen lived in Kabul, Afghanistan, for a couple of years and observed the subservient role of women in that society and her own. When she returned to the United States, she saw that many women were questioning "the expectations they had grown up with." Nilsen chose the study of sexism in the English language as a quieter means of examining women's role in society. She discovered that language and society are so intertwined that she could not avoid facing social issues head on.

2. Nilsen makes the following points:
   a. English words derived from the name of a person: A very large number of everyday words have come into modern English from the names of men. A very much smaller number of words have entered the language from the names of women, and most of them come from Greek mythology (7, 8, and 9).
   b. geographical names: Many American place names refer to women's sexual features, especially their breasts (10 and 11).
   c. pairs of words, one masculine and the other feminine: Often "the feminine word has acquired sexual connotations while the masculine word retains a serious businesslike aura" (12), as <u>callboy/call girl</u> (12), <u>sir/madam</u> (12), and other pairs illustrate. Furthermore, in masculine-feminine pairs of words, the masculine word "is considered the base, with some kind of feminine suffix

being added" (14), and the masculine words appear in far more compounds than do the feminine words.

d. the use of words referring to foods, plants, and animals in connection with women: Women in our society "are expected to play a passive or weak role" (19); our language reveals this expectation by its large number of words describing in terms of foods or something to eat (25), plants (26), and pets rather than aggressive animals (27).

e. the first names given to male and female infants: Girls are much more likely to be given names like Ivy, Rose, Ruby, Jewel, Pearl, Flora, etc., while boys are given names describing active roles such as Martin (warlike), Raymond (wise protection), and so on (24 and 26).

f. the use of Ms.: Women who ask to be identified as Ms. rather than as Miss or Mrs. are protesting against being defined in terms of their relationship to a man (21 and 22).

g. dictionary entries concerning famous women: Even women who are famous in their own right are almost always identified in dictionary entries in terms of their relationships to some male-- husband, brother, father, even lover. Such listings are not given for men (21).

h. positive and negative connotations connected with the concepts "masculine" and "feminine": Nilsen argues that there are many positive connotations connected with the concept of masculine, "while there are either trivial or negative connotations connected with the corresponding feminine concept" (28). She discusses this idea at length in paragraphs 29 through 35.

3. If the purpose of a dictionary is, in fact, to lay out how the language is actually used and not to pass judgments on that usage, then dictionary makers cannot be faulted for including definitions that betray cultural biases. Students' opinions on this matter may vary, but they should be encouraged to explain the reasoning behind their attitudes.

4. In paragraphs 15 and 18, Nilsen reveals that only in the areas of sex and marriage do women appear more important than men.

5. In paragraph 36, Nilsen lists several changes she has seen in the language over the last twenty years: the increased use of inclusive language; the use of she/he or they when the gender is unknown or unclear; guidelines issued by publishers to help writers use language that is fair to both sexes; women listed in newspapers by their name instead of their husband's; business letters that begin with "Dear Colleagues" and "Dear Reader" instead of "Dear Sir"; the elimination of nouns that add ess to render them feminine; and the use of both men's and women's names for hurricanes. These changes show Nilsen that "sexism is not something

existing independently in American English. . . . It exists in people's minds"
(37).

Instead of being the alternative to both <u>Mrs.</u> and <u>Miss</u> that it was
intended to be, <u>Ms.</u> has replaced <u>Miss</u> to become a catchall business title for
women.

Writing Topics (p. 387)

1. Students should be reminded that as they explain how improvements
can be brought about they will need to provide specific examples to illustrate
exactly how changes can occur. You may also wish to analyze how Nilsen
has incorporated the discussion of examples into her essay before students
approach their own.

2. The opposition to women's attempts to change language is in part a
reaction to change itself; many people fear and distrust change. Other
opponents feel that the suggested changes are silly and either are not
needed or would have no effect. We do not think that the opposition is
justified, because many attitudes and prejudices are unconsciously
transmitted and reinforced by language.

The most effective technique employed by an opposition is ridicule, as
Jonathan Swift and other satirists have long known. Some changes in
language would be silly (for example, <u>hurricane</u> to <u>himicane</u>), and even
though no serious feminists support them, opponents make fun of them and
ignore the serious sexual biases of English.

On the Subway

Sharon Olds

Questions for Study and Discussion (p. 389)

1. The speaker's first impressions of the boy lead to fear, apprehension,
concern, and worry for her own safety. As the poem continues, she
becomes more sympathetic to his situation. After understanding how he
looks to her and how that makes her feel in the first part of the poem, the
author progresses to speculation about how she looks to him and how that
makes him feel.

2. The fact that the boy is a black youth in a society dominated by
whites is underscored by the simile of his black sneakers restricted by white
laces. The pattern of the laces makes her think of the regular or patterned
sears left by a whipping. The simile describes his life as one that is
restrained and not free; he is held back by people of another race. The
speaker begins to understand the boy's plight and thinks how she is one of
those laces.

82

3. In lines 9 to 11, the red clothing, "like the inside of the body /
exposed," stands for the boy's vulnerability. In lines 24 to 26, the "black
cotton" represents how the black youth has become the type of person who
takes the heat, or blame, for many societal problems, especially in cities.
The references to breaking, in lines 29 to 31, stand for the fragility of both
the boy and the author; the references represent the threat of violence that
each character experiences.
4. The boy is "raw" in that he is young, untamed, and threatening, at
least in the author's eyes.
5. The speaker seems to indicate that because she is white, she is
better off than the black boy, perhaps because white society exploits the
black population, especially the young. Her life is better, more privileged,
and has more opportunities than his. The boy is in the speaker's power in
the sense that the white speaker defines the boy and the situation. She, on
the other hand, feels caught in his power because of her fear of being
mugged. Both the exploitation and the fear of blacks make her feel guilty
and vulnerable.
6. Student responses will differ.

Writing Topics (p. 389)

1. This topic picks up from question 6 above. Student responses will
tend to focus on the disadvantages of being a certain race, creed, or other
characteristic, rather than on the advantages, especially since young people
often hone in on the ways people take advantage of them or take them for
granted. Have students identify stereotypes from television and movies,
noting how things have changed, or not, over time. Pairing students might
be useful here; ask the pairs to compare reality and stereotypes.
2. Encourage students to go beyond knee-jerk reactions or responding
with political platitudes. As with the previous writing topic, students will
react vociferously once they are made to feel comfortable expressing
themselves honestly, which may be the biggest challenge of this
assignment.

The Yellow Wallpaper

Charlotte Perkins Gilman

Questions for Study and Discussion (p. 404)

1. The heroine tires from writing, entertaining, traveling, "controlling"
herself, following the pattern in the wallpaper, and finally even from trying to
think clearly. In short, she is emotionally weary and is suffering a severe

depression.

2. The paper is drab. It lacks a pattern or a plan, as does the heroine's life. The two patterns represent the inner and outer selves of women of that era. Specifically, the front pattern represents the attitudes and behavior proper to a "good wife," while the back pattern represents the imaginative, emotional self that women of Gilman's time were expected to keep "under control."

3. The woman describes her husband first as "practical," and having "no patience with faith," but also as a nurturing and caring man. She respects him and does what she can to appease him without making any real judgment about how his treatment of her contributes to her illness. Later, however, she grows suspicious of John and even a "little afraid." He seems "queer" to her, but she attributes his behavior to the wallpaper. Finally, he becomes the enemy and she must free herself, "in spite of" him and Jane.

4. The wife is suffering a nervous breakdown, either as the result of postpartum depression or from the effects of a sheltered and oppressive life. But because her condition is grounded in mental rather than physical causes, and because her husband has removed all that he believes would cause her to suffer, he cannot believe that her condition is serious.

5. The husband is very nurturing, but acts more as a father than a husband. He says, "What is it, little girl?" when he catches her up late at night, and refers to her childlike "imaginative power and habit of story-making." Meanwhile, the wife makes reference to her need for stimulation, a change of scene, and secrecy. She is stronger and more in touch with her needs than her husband gives her credit for.

6. As the story progresses, the wife becomes more and more involved with the paper, which of course is a metaphor for her condition. At first she merely dislikes it. Then it takes on human qualities and she sees things moving in it. Soon the paper is all she can think about. The people around her change from nurturing to sinister in her eyes and the room she abhorred becomes her refuge. Her tragic decline is marked by the repetition of words such as "nervous" and by phrases such as: "I cry at nothing" (90); "There are things in that paper that nobody knows but me, or ever will" (122); "torturing" (145); and "I wonder if they all come out of that wall-paper as I did!" (246). Gilman moves the story along at a fast enough pace so that we see the swift, yet smooth decline of the wife.

7. The word creep connotes sneaking. In the context of the story, the women "creep" to avoid detection and the forced return to a despised way of life.

8. Just as she is secretive about her writing, the woman is secretive about her fantasies about the wallpaper. Nothing about the wallpaper is revealed to the husband, and she does not tell him that she writes. Both activities are symbolic and real manifestations of her crumbling independence.

84

9. The woman soon grows to like the room because of the wallpaper. The change in attitude signifies her "going over the edge." She is afraid to go outside because the "woman" is out there. As the woman creeps, so would she, and it is embarrassing to have others see you "creep" in the daylight. The woman escapes from her husband into madness and so achieves a final, terrible victory.

<u>Writing Topics (p. 404)</u>

1. As a prewriting activity you may want to discuss postpartum depression and how a feminist would react to someone blaming the heroine's condition on a hormone imbalance. It may also be useful to discuss Gilman's purpose in writing this story.

2. Answering the list of questions will serve to focus students on one topic for their assignment and to organize their thoughts. Students may also wish to consider how Gilman's ideas have informed feminism today and how they are found in contemporary feminist writing.

<u>Language and Persuasion</u>

Politics and the English Language

George Orwell

<u>Questions for Study and Discussion (p. 416)</u>

1. As Orwell has it, bad politics--the unthinking reiteration of the party line, the defense of the indefensible, and the like--makes for foggy and stale language. Most would agree. But he goes on to argue that such language in turn can be an obstacle to honesty and sincerity in politics. (See paragraph 2.)

2. Orwell defines dying metaphors (5), operators or verbal false limbs (6), pretentious diction (7), and meaningless words (8), all of them hackneyed, prefabricated devices that substitute for actual thinking. He explains each by providing numerous common examples.

3. Prefabricated houses are not chosen or built because they reflect the buyer's taste. They are look-alike, mass-produced structures that have no individuality. Similarly, prefabricated phrases are "long strips of words which have already been set in order by someone else" (11) and release a person from the responsibility of choosing words that express an exact meaning. In both prefabricated houses and prefabricated language, quality is sacrificed for convenience and economy of effort.

4. Students should be asked to consider exactly what is being compared

to what in each case, then to analyze why Orwell thought each particular comparison appropriate to its context.

    a. "A huge dump of worn-out metaphors" suggests a trash heap of objects that were once useful but no longer work--an obviously appropriate figure of speech, that also implies that people who use such metaphors are picking over the trash and garbage of language.

    b. Used tea leaves, again, are garbage, and the figure of speech suggests that "stale" phrases "choke" off the flow of communication just as the leaves choke off the flow of water out of the sink.

    c. Euphemism, of which Orwell considers the inflated style an example, is meant to soften the impact of sharp, unpleasant truths. Snow, of course, softens the sharp outlines of objects. And both euphemism and snow succeed in "covering up all the details."

    d. Both the politician and the cuttlefish (or squid) are to be seen as escaping from danger and covering their tracks. The comparison is all the more amusing because both may use ink, though ejecting it from different orifices.

    e. Cavalry horses are so thoroughly trained that they recognize and obey bugle calls as a conditioned reflex. Orwell's simile is appropriate because it suggests that the "familiar dreary pattern" of the pamphleteer's words is absolutely rigid and unvarying, like a military formation, and also that the number of patterns available to that writer, like the number of bugle calls used by an army, is extremely limited.

    5. Orwell's essay contains remarkably few stale or vague phrases. In paragraph 1, "it is generally assumed," "so the argument runs," and "it follows that" are overly familiar devices. In paragraph 2, Orwell uses an unwarranted construction: "It is clear that." In fact, Orwell frequently begins his sentences with the impersonal construction "it is," for example in paragraph 12--"it is broadly true that" and "it will generally be found"--and this is a rather wordy way to get a sentence going. "Pad" in paragraph 6 is a metaphor that he must often have seen in print. But these lapses are few and minor, and his acknowledgment has the effect of disarming readers and convincing them that he is modest, reasonable, and aware of the difficulty of avoiding ready-made constructions.

    6. Orwell's final rule underlines a central point: that good writing emphasizes meaning, not obedience to any set of rules, even his own. As he says in paragraph 18, his point "has nothing to do with correct grammar and syntax, which are of no importance as long as one makes one's meaning

clear. . . . What is above all needed is to let the meaning choose the word, and not the other way about."

<u>Writing Topics (p. 417)</u>

1. Situations such as this topic outlines come up in most people's daily lives, and they are generally dealt with through white lies (or lies that are not so white). Handling such situations in an honest way, yet still avoiding a premature or damaging answer, is problematic because it usually reveals that a person is holding something back. This issue of practical ethics is surprisingly knotty, as suggested by Sissela Bok's <u>Lying: Moral Choice in Public and Private Life</u> (1978).

2. Students should have no difficulty locating examples in the newspaper, especially in <u>The New York Times</u>, which regularly prints political speeches in their entirety. The Iran-Contra or the savings and loan hearings revealed many such abuses of language.

3. The purpose of Newspeak was to manipulate truth, to distort history, and to control the minds of its users. Thus, Newspeak is a fictionalized extension of the tendencies toward manipulative language that Orwell warned against in "Politics and the English Language." Interestingly, the people of <u>1984</u> began using Newspeak voluntarily and more and more frequently, pushing ahead the projected timetable for making it the standard language of Oceania.

Propaganda: How Not to Be Bamboozled

Donna Woolfolk Cross

<u>Questions for Study and Discussion (p. 428)</u>

1. According to Cross, the propagandist can influence our thinking by "appealing to our emotions, distracting our attention . . . , misleading us with logic that may appear to be reasonable but is in fact faulty and deceiving" (46), and using testimonials or endorsements from public figures who, in effect, we let "make our decisions <u>for us</u>" (50).

2. The testimonial that "consists in having some loved or respected person give a statement of support (testimonial) for a given product or idea" (47) is the device most often used by propagandists. Advertising abounds with examples of testimonials: for example, the model Linda Evangelista endorsing a brand of makeup, or retired professional athletes praising a particular beer. Politicians also use endorsements, whether from other politicians or from television and movie actors, or even from carefully selected "ordinary" citizens.

3. Cross first defines the device, then proceeds by giving at least two examples, one involving "Senator Yakalot." In her closing paragraph for each section she explains the device's intent and tells us how to defend ourselves against it and think for ourselves. Cross seems to organize her propaganda devices by beginning with the most obvious techniques (name-calling, glittering generalities) and moving to the more "insidious," easily overlooked ones.

4. Cross attributes familiar propagandistic phrases to Senator Yakalot (yak is slang for talk), a fictitious politician who stands for all the real politicians who have used these demagogic tactics.

5. Cross compares people who support a popular cause with lemmings, who are driven by instinct to rush into deep water and drown themselves. The analogy is apt because both the lemmings and the masses of people are operating by sheer instinct and not by reason--and, often, against their own best interests. The analogy is not altogether accurate, however, since lemmings are genetically compelled to drown themselves, while people can decide to hold back from the crowd.

Writing Topics (p. 428)

1. Students may use fundraising literature and advertising by UNICEF, the American Cancer Society, and overseas relief organizations as examples. Undoubtedly, such propaganda appeals to people's emotions rather than to their reason and seeks to make them feel strongly about a cause and perhaps to overlook legitimate issues such as how much of their money is spent not only helping people but also on paying the fundraisers. However, except perhaps among tax accountants, the decision to give is often unselfish and emotional, and it is hard to imagine an effective charitable campaign that is not mainly emotional in appeal.

2. When attempting to persuade people, propaganda is difficult to avoid using and often has considerably more "crowd appeal" than does logical argument. Glittering generalities, ad hominem arguments, begging the question, and false dilemmas are particularly common pitfalls. Students who think themselves above using propaganda will find this an enlightening exercise--and all will find it essential as preparation for college work.

Advertising's Fifteen Basic Appeals

Jib Fowles

1. We do not agree that buyers have become stoutly resistant to advertisements. Buyers are aware, to a certain extent, of the morals being inflicted on them and some of the emotions being appealed to. But there are some appeals and claims that buyers are not aware of. Students will no doubt have many examples of their own gullibility.

2. Fowles's tone must seem somewhat overbearing to the student unfamiliar with psychology. His references to some of the great psychologists would mean nothing to such a reader. Although Fowles seems proud of his discovery of fifteen appeals, readers get lost in the process. Still, they may question Fowles's downgrading of the works of Maslow, Murray, and McClelland.

3. In Fowles's extensive explanation of the process that went into finding his appeals, he borrows ideas from well-known psychologists. He also uses many examples to support his thesis. He is convincing as a professor who knows a great deal about psychology; however, he tempers that knowledge by refuting thinkers who are at least as well respected as he is. We do not find all of his examples to be thoroughly convincing.

4. The emotional appeal is found in the artwork.

5. Fowles suggests that Florence Henderson is the main appeal in Wesson Oil commercials, although the food plays an equally major role. The sight of fried chicken and French fries soaking in Wesson Oil appeals to a simple, basic need, the desire for good, hot, greasy food. Most food ads rely on the sight of mouth-watering food to make the sale. Fowles's assessment of ad writers' intentions may be correct; however, it is possible that consumers are perhaps not so easily influenced. More than any other product, food is subject to tests that have an immediate and definite influence over the consumer. They are less likely to be fooled just because a food product is endorsed by a perceived motherly image or has a history.

6. Although public protest has at times forced advertisers to pull campaigns, mere opposition to an ad might not necessarily bring it to a halt, unless, of course, that opposition affects sales. Ad writers may be satisfied with ads that get attention, good or bad; publicity is the whole idea.

1. It may be helpful for students to get more information on subliminal advertising before beginning this assignment. Students can find additional

information under the heading Subliminal Advertising in the library's subject catalogue or various indexes.

2. As a prewriting activity you may review the elements of division and classification. Once the assignment is completed you may want to share some of the more witty responses with the entire class.

Inaugural Address, 1993

Bill Clinton

<u>Questions for Study and Discussion (p. 450)</u>

1. Clinton stresses that the old order has passed responsibility to the next generation of American leaders. This duty will be carried forward with a spirit of renewal, hard work, and service. The new generation will reinvent America by invigorating past principles such as grasping responsibility, meeting challenges, and cooperating in a sense of community. Students will probably focus on those aspects that are personal challenges, especially the remarks made directly to them in paragraph 23.

2. Each time a new president is inaugurated, the person brings in new advisers, policies, and ideas for government. The "mystery" may be in the fact that, unlike in many other countries, the transfer of power happens without bloodshed or civil war; there is a peaceful transition of the power and authority of the presidential office. The image of spring captures the spirit of rebirth, freshness, newness, and promise of the new administration.

3. Clinton sees several parts of the definition: an entrepreneurial spirit, a willingness to meet challenges with gusto, creativity, and dedication. In paragraph 8, he calls Americans "a restless, questing, hopeful people," adding, "our people have always mustered the determination to construct from these crises [the American Revolution, Civil War, and Great Depression] the pillars of our history." Students may tend either to be very stirred by the rhetoric or to have a very jaded reaction, saying that Clinton's words ring hollow to them.

4. To Clinton, boldness, dedication to service, and willingness to band together as a community in mutual self-sacrifice help Americans exploit chances for improvement. As he says in paragraph 12, "We must do what America does best: offer more opportunity to all and demand more responsibility from all." Clinton feels that following this manifesto will lead to what is best for Americans. Students should ask themselves what they would add to this list of America's strengths, or else give examples from this list of traits that are evident in their school, home, neighborhood, or service activity.

5. Clinton's tone is without question exhortatory and inspirational. His

diction is full of images of renewal and his pace is punctuated by short, crisp sentences. His use of "America" as a soaring, shining symbol adds to his upbeat tone, as well as his calls to action: "let us," "we must," and "we will."

<u>Writing Topics (p. 451)</u>

1. Students should take time to think about the different purposes for speeches. The goal of a speech can be to inspire, inform, entertain, or a combination of these purposes. Students might consider whether an inaugural address ought to be specific to the occasion. As an exercise in considering the different goals of writing, students might be asked to write a speech that informs an audience about a topic, and then to write another that inspires the same audience on the same topic. In order to make this assignment real, ask students to select a topic related to their school experience, such as whether grades should be abolished.

2. Picking up on the previous exercise, students should think about the ways in which different historical circumstances dictate appropriately varied responses. They might compare the strong tone of Lincoln's first inaugural address with the more conciliatory notes he hit in his second. They might also discuss how the style of the speech fits the speaker, imagining Kennedy's words, for example, in Bush's mouth. Whether students feel alienated or included by these speeches can also infuse this discussion with an understanding of how keeping an audience in mind affects a speechwriter's choices.

3. Have the students both explain and exhort in the same speech. They should also bear in mind that a speech written to be heard will be composed differently than an essay meant to be read. They might write an essay and a speech on the same topic to see the contrast. Have them pay particular attention to the sounds of language in the silent mind of the writer and in the mouth of the speech giver.

When Language Dies: 1993 Nobel Prize for Literature Acceptance Speech

Toni Morrison

<u>Questions for Study and Discussion (p. 458)</u>

1. Morrison takes this story to be an imagined discussion about the place of language in a society: what it once meant and what it could mean. She says the bird represents language; the old woman stands for a tradition of writing that respected language and revered it so much that it used language properly and imaginatively; and the young people symbolize a new

generation that can make of language what it wants. They can continue with an empty tradition that made violent use of language for oppressive ends, or choose to reinvigorate language with a fresh approach that expands language for benevolent goals.

2. The young people were reprimanded because they mocked the old woman; they did not accord her the proper respect. The old woman points out how they sacrificed language in order to parade "their power and her helplessness" (10).

3. In paragraph 11, Morrison uses the phrase "statist language" to refer to language that has become an instrument of repression and censorship. It is language that oppressive governments use to maintain power and beat back challenges. Such language is dead and lifeless because it lacks color and vividness, yet, the author laments, "it is not without effect for it actively thwarts the intellect, stalls conscience, suppresses human potential." This type of official language is rigid and static.

4. Many people are responsible for the "systematic looting of language," according to Morrison. In paragraph 13, she names as guilty parties government institutions, the "mindless media," scholars, scientists, lawyers, and racists.

5. The story of the Tower of Babel comes from the Bible, Genesis 11:1-9. The story is about men who began to build a tower that would reach to heaven. God, angry that they presumed they could achieve such a goal, made the men speak different languages so they could not communicate and therefore could not complete their project. The tower tumbled. Morrison does not follow the conventional wisdom that interprets the story to mean that one language would have been a good thing that would have led to the completion of the tower. She holds that a single language is limiting. She thinks that a multitude of languages, and therefore a multitude of perspectives and viewpoints, is preferable.

6. Morrison means that life itself is not easy to comprehend. Language, by definition limited, represents only an attempt to describe processes and stages of life that cannot ever be fully captured in words. The attempt to do so, however, allows people to stretch language and expand its limits. In the end, though, human emotion goes beyond human potential to dress feelings in words. This is a paradox that must be understood, especially by writers, Morrison argues.

7. The questions are in paragraph 23: "Is the bird we hold living or dead?" "Could some one tell us what is life? What is death?" These fundamental questions recur throughout the next several paragraphs. It appears that what the young people are really seeking is an answer to the question "What is the meaning of life?" since they recognize that the old blind woman is, in fact, wise and not feeble-minded. Morrison seems to be asking the young people to use the "bird" in their hands, which represents language, to seek their own answers to these questions.

8. The old woman, hearing the questions turn into a narrative about slaves in a wagon, realizes that these young people are maturing. They understand that they have basic questions. This pleases the old woman. She can trust the young people because they understand the gift of language they possess. What they have "done--together" is share an appreciation of the value of that gift.

Writing Topics (p. 458)

1. This assignment will probably bring up many pleasant memories for students, who should be encouraged to capture the magical language and playtimes of their childhood. When they come up with a memory they find hard to express, challenge them to take Morrison's advice to try to capture the "ineffable" but also to appreciate the limits of language. Students might consider the cultural or gender differences in the childhood stories they heard, or how their use of language changed as they moved from childhood to young adulthood.

2. Students who often daydream or enjoy science fiction or other fantasies might try to create their own version of a complete society. As models, they might read selections from classic examples of such fiction, such as C. S. Lewis's Narnia Chronicle (especially The Lion, the Witch, and the Wardrobe) and J. R. R. Tolkien's Ring series (especially The Hobbit).

Harrison Bergeron

Kurt Vonnegut, Jr.

Questions for Study and Discussion (p. 465)

1. When students take a close look at the story they will be surprised at how little the world it depicts differs from the world of today. For example, people then talk much as they do today; they still watch television, ballet still exists as does canned beer; and Diana Moon Glampers arms herself with a double-barreled ten-gauge shotgun. The only difference is that in 2081 equality of ability has been imposed by handicapping the talented. Vonnegut's intention is clearly to focus the reader's attention wholly on the theme of his story--total equality. Had he created a more futuristic world, he would have run the risk of diverting the reader's attention from that theme.

2. George refers to the competitive past as the "dark ages" because he believes that the present (2081) is a more enlightened and civilized time. Handicapping eliminates the ability to excel and thus makes competition pointless if not impossible. In this world, any exceptional and underhandicapped person (like Harrison) is dangerous because the society of

2081 would "fall all apart" (33)--or, as nearly happens, because such a person might try to become an absolute ruler.

3. Some specific handicaps that people have to wear are sashweights, bags of birdshot, masks and clown noses, and receivers so that they can be "buzzed" with assorted noises to prevent the possibility of connected thought. These handicaps are essentially comical and suggest the work of a fertile but odd imagination. That the people of 2081 accept such indignities reveals how conditioned and unthinking they have become.

4. One reason that Vonnegut made Harrison Bergeron a fourteen-year-old boy is to show us a character whose mind and body are still developing and whose handicaps therefore need constant monitoring. His first appearance in paragraph 54 suggests something of the child, but otherwise there is little that is childish about him--he is, after all, exceptional.

5. Shifting to fantasy at this point in the story allows Vonnegut to create an extreme contrast to the flat, equalized world he has been describing up to this point. (And perhaps, after all, by 2081 an exceptional human being would be able to do what Harrison does.) A less fantastic climax might have been more believable, but then the story is not meant to be believable; it is a parable on the theme of equality.

6. Diana Moon Glampers, as the person who assigns handicaps and enforces them, is the true ruler of 2081 society. Her job requires careful assessments of everyone's ability and the measured handicapping of each person to achieve a balanced equality, and when the system is threatened she takes direct, calculated, effective action. Hazel thinks, in paragraph 18, that she'd "make a good Handicapper General," but immediately reveals that she is too soft-hearted and probably too dull-witted for the job. It's notable that the handicaps Diana Moon Glampers imposes are comical and reductive not only of capability but of dignity as well, and also that she is evidently empowered to kill violators of the handicapping laws without a trial.

7. If all men are created equal, as the Declaration of Independence asserts, they are certainly not created average. Equality, as defended in American tradition and law, is a matter of equal standing before the law and equal opportunity to try to succeed--not of equal talent, or equal success regardless of talent. In Vonnegut's story the social ideal is not equality but averageness, which requires that the above-average be brought down and the below-average (like the radio announcer in paragraphs 37 to 38) be elevated to positions they are ill-equipped to fill.

Writing Topics (p. 466)

1. Exploring American attitudes toward exceptional people can be enlightening. Schoolchildren tend to admire athletically gifted classmates rather than the brainy ones, and many carry that prejudice into adult life--evidently we would rather feel relatively clumsy than relatively stupid.

Political leaders attract not only enthusiastic followers but assassins as well; the very rich excite curiosity, envy, and admiration simply because of their wealth. The attitude Vonnegut satirizes in "Harrison Bergeron," that of wanting to bring exceptional people down to one's level (though not, of course, to reduce oneself to a still lower level!), has long appealed to those who think such equality particularly democratic, and may explain the success of some very mediocre people in public life. But of course too much respect for the exceptional person, especially the exceptional politician, can lead to dictatorship and disaster, as in Germany in the 1930s.

2. Those who support or oppose the various programs mentioned here may not have thought of them in quite the terms we pose. Even if a person favors affirmative action on the grounds of fairness, for example, it may mean that one's education, or one's open-heart surgery, is being conducted by a less qualified, less able person than would otherwise have been the case.

3. Both Vonnegut and Auden are satirizing imaginary societies that are much like our own and that take the ordinary man as the norm. In both works the society values conformity highly and places no value on individuality or on the individual's feelings and aspirations. In Auden's poem, however, the average, "unknown citizen" is determined by statistical means, whereas in "Harrison Bergeron" average citizens are created through handicapping.

6 / Cultural Encounters

Chief Red Jacket Responds to the Reverend Mr. Cram

Chief Red Jacket

Questions for Study and Discussion (p. 472)

1. The missionary comes to these people without having any real knowledge of their religion or how they practice it, yet he assumes they are not worshiping correctly. The missionary claims they have never worshiped the Great Spirit properly and therefore they have "been in great errors and darkness" (5) for their whole lives. He assumes that they will worship the Christian God if he opens their eyes to their error.

2. Red Jacket rejects the proposal by telling the story of what happened to the Indians the last time they trusted the white man. He begins by explaining how happy and peaceful they were before the missionary's forefathers came. Red Jacket then goes on to explain that these visitors took land and possessions without giving anything back until it got to the

point where the Indians had virtually nowhere to go. Red Jacket's arguments are sound because, although they are passionate words, they are an accurate account of how the country was progressively taken from the Indians.

3. It would seem that the missionary was willing to hear objections to his proposal only if his position remained defensible; however, Red Jacket's arguments were so convincing, the missionary had nothing to say in return that would contradict the truths Red Jacket presented.

4. Red Jacket says his people will reconsider the white man's religion when they see the white man following the practices they preach. He says, "If we find it does them good, makes them honest and less disposed to cheat Indians; we will then consider again of what you have said" (25).

5. As the Indians approach the Reverend Mr. Cram, Red Jacket says that they hope the Great Spirit will protect him on his journey, returning him safely to his friends. Cram refuses to shake their hands, saying there is no fellowship between them since they did not accept his religion. He associates their religion with the devil. The smiles of the Indians only help to prove that the white man makes no attempt to understand the ideals that make up their religion.

6. The missionary refuses the handshake because he does not want the Indians to think that he agrees with them in any way. The Indians, however, give no sign that they believe a handshake signifies agreement--to them it seems merely a gesture of friendship. Cram's apology for the slight was expectedly insincere given his lack of understanding for the Indian people and their ways.

Writing Topics (p. 473)

1. These letters will depend on the students' views and knowledge of the history between the Indian and the white man. Some may feel the Indians should have accepted circumstances since they were outnumbered, whereas others may agree with Red Jacket and believe that the white man has brought only harm to the Indian people. In order to update the exercise, students might be encouraged to compare this selection to the presentation of encounters between Indians and whites in films such as Dances with Wolves.

2. A discussion may include a comparison of the misunderstanding between Cram and Red Jacket and the clashes of views that we read about in the headlines today. Have students consider local or personal examples of cultural exchanges, such as racially or religiously mixed marriages. Discuss positive and negative aspects of such encounters with examples of both good and bad results.

In Search of Bruce Lee's Grave

Shanlon Wu

Questions for Study and Discussion (p. 476)

1. Bruce Lee was a martial arts expert who became a star of action films and a Hollywood celebrity. He was Wu's first boyhood hero and a positive Asian role model.

2. In paragraph 3, Wu notes that Hop Sing, the houseboy on the TV series "Bonanza" was an Asian caricature who did nothing to contradict the stereotype of Asians as deferential servants; in fact, he contributed to this picture. Wu goes so far as to describe Hop Sing as "that most pathetic of Asian characters."

3. We know from paragraph 6 that Wu's parents are intellectuals and immigrants. His childhood differed from theirs because, growing up in China, they were members of the majority race and part of the mainstream, dominant culture, whereas Wu was an outsider in the United States. Because of this essential difference in experiences, his parents understood that it would probably have been detrimental to impose their childhood on Wu: It would only have made the boy feel even more alienated and isolated from the society in which he grew up.

4. Wu was trying to emulate Bruce Lee; in so doing, Wu was not being true to himself, but trying to fit the model of a movie star. Wu discovered that he had to find who he was as an individual. Instruction on how to live could not come from the movies because movies are not real life. Wu needed to learn how to compete in actual circumstances where he was not the dominating character, as Lee had been in his films. Lee's movies, in other words, were an artificial reality and, as such, could not prepare Wu to live and work as a professional in the school and work environments in which he found himself.

5. In paragraphs 10 and 11, Wu discusses the heroic efforts of the 442d Regimental Combat Team, a U.S. all-Japanese unit in World War II. General Minoru Genda, the man who planned the Japanese attack on Pearl Harbor, was another of Wu's heroes (18-19). These models gave Wu images of power, pride, and accomplishment, but, as with Lee, they fell short as adequate role models because their acts took place on heroic, even epic, levels. Wu had to be true to himself in daily experiences.

6. Visiting the grave was emotional for Wu because it brought home to him how his search for a hero ended up helping him define himself. As he notes in paragraphs 22 to 24, Lee pointed the way for Wu that ultimately led him to himself. "Seeing his grave," Wu says in paragraph 22, "I understand how large the hole in my life has been and how desperately I'd sought to fill

it." The search for the grave stood for his wider search for role models and for himself.

7. Wu was forced to fall back on his own abilities, creativity, imagination, and resources. He had to define a vision for himself and pursue it so that, in the end, he could be his own man and, more significantly for the essay, his own hero.

Writing Topics (p. 477)

1. Depending especially on the race of the students and the part of the country or town in which they live, work, or attend school, student responses will cover a wide range of experiences. A prewriting exercise might ask them to list what they see as aspects of a majority and a minority culture; they can then determine where they fit in. Do they fit in differently in various settings? Are they sometimes part of the majority culture and other times part of the minority? The writing topic itself, however, should go beyond these notes. A thoughtful anecdote that typifies the struggle for identity should be the goal of the essay, rather than a laundry list of observations.

2. Students can discuss whether music, movie, or sports stars should or should not be heroes. When these people fall from grace, is it their fault or the fault of those who put them on a pedestal in the first place? Ask students to consider everyday heroes or even themselves as heroes. Should there be any heroes at all or should people work to build themselves up as their own heroes?

Talking in the New Land

Edite Cunha

Questions for Study and Discussion (p. 487)

1. Maria Edite dos Anjos Cunha's name derives from several sources. "Maria" is the traditional Portuguese prefix for all girls' names, in reverence for the Virgin Mary (1). "Edite" is her godmother's name, and "dos Anjos" is a family name from the maternal side (2). "Cunha" is her father's name and signifies her father's family history and origins (3). The significance of Cunha's name, as she puts it, is that "through it I knew exactly who I was" (4). Her name fused all of the elements of her identify (her nationality, culture, religion, mother, and father).

2. Mrs. Donahue said that she wanted to change Cunha's name to conform to the American convention of referring to people by only two names, and because it would be easier to pronounce (presumably for

Americans) (10). It could be that Mrs. Donahue, as a Portuguese immigrant herself, had negative experiences in confronting these issues of naming when she first arrived in the United States and had meant to make Cunha's adjustment easier by changing her name.

3. At first Cunha was frustrated by Mrs. Donahue and resisted her attempts to call her by her new name (14). Eventually, Cunha writes, "I grew to love Mrs. Donahue" (16) and was reluctant to leave her class (17). The irony in paragraph 6 is that Mrs. Donahue's name seemed unpronounceable to Cunha, yet it was Mrs. Donahue who would change Cunha's name to something Cunha herself could not pronounce; the further irony of course is that Mrs. Donahue was Portuguese.

4. When Mrs. Donahue first started trying to teach Cunha how to pronounce her new name, "she looked hideous" (12) to Cunha. However, Cunha later describes Mrs. Donahue with a kind of affection, noting her smile, her clothing, and her "oddity"--her legs of different lengths (15). Cunha "grew to love Mrs. Donahue" because she danced with the class and because "the oddity of Mrs. Donahue's classroom had draped itself over me like a warm safe cloak" (17). Mrs. Donahue's oddities are important to Cunha and are ironic in that Mrs. Donahue probably was not aware of them and would have avoided them if she had been.

5. The irony of Mrs. Donahue's insistence on Cunha's correct pronunciation of Miss Laitinen's name is that Mrs. Donahue refused to pronounce Maria Edite dos Anjos Cunha's name correctly.

6. Since it must have seemed to Cunha as though everyone relied on her to translate for them, and she took her interpretive responsibility so seriously, she often found herself embroiled in the disputes of others. She was a sensitive person who took personally the feelings that others were actually trying to convey to each other, and no doubt others' frustrations were indeed taken out on her to some extent.

7. There are several purposes. First, Cunha is clearly seeking sympathy from her audience. She is not self-centered or pitiable, however, because, second, the author wants people to understand her situation, not change it or take it away. Finally, she probably wants to remind readers that immigrant stories are still being "written": Immigrants are alive today, not merely part of textbook history.

8. Following the Division of Employment Security scene, Cunha relates that she knew that her father would have stayed and argued with the claims agent if he had been able to speak English, and she suspected that "he thought it was my fault we couldn't have money. And I myself wasn't so sure that wasn't true" (85). In the scene with the woman wanting the dishes back, Cunha was caught between her father's stubbornness and the sympathy she had for the woman's request. Both incidents exemplify the excruciating positions in which Cunha was put by her father simply because oho oould epeak English. Looking at the way she describes the negative

aspects of "Talking in the New Land," there is little wonder why she says, "I hated myself for having learned to speak English" (139).

Writing Topics (p. 487)

1. Students recollections of their difficulties in learning foreign languages are likely to emphasize one or more of the following areas of language learning: acquiring a new vocabulary, including idiomatic expressions; learning the grammar of a new language; and, learning how to pronounce unfamiliar sounds. Though many students may not have experienced being placed in a schoolroom where the language was foreign to them, they may have encountered situations on vacations or during travels where they did not speak or understand the native language. For those who have, discuss in class whether they can identify with Cunha's description of how foreign sounds affected her. Equally interesting might be a discussion of any students' experiences of frustration of being able to speak a foreign language among others who are dependent upon their translations.

2. First- or second-generation immigrants will probably side with Cunha, as will anyone with a strong ethnic heritage. Moving beyond proper names, students might also consider nicknames: whether they chose them or were labeled, how they feel about them, what they reveal (fairly or otherwise), and why they hurt or fill them with pride.

3. As a prewriting discussion for this assignment, ask your students to relate what role their families have played in the development of their language skills. Find out, for example, how many of them were read aloud to as children and whether they feel it had any effect on their facility with language. Or discover what, if any, similarities exist in the experiences that have contributed greatly to students' learning language skills. Your discussion may lead students into areas of thought they can follow up on in their essays.

On Being White, Female, and Born in Bensonhurst

Marianna De Marco Torgovnick

Questions for Study and Discussion (p. 499)

1. Torgovnick repeatedly refers to the ways in which social structures and lifestyles repeat themselves in Bensonhurst: Italian families quickly replace others that move out of the neighborhood (2) or move only a few blocks away (12); people pass the evenings sitting on their stoops (4); people pass the evenings sitting on their stoops (4); the same sign soliciting donations for the local church sits on the church property year after year (6);

her parents' apartment rarely changes (7); and young women follow a pattern of secretarial school, marriage, and children (25).

2. She understands the strong feelings of territoriality and proprietary "ownership" of Bensonhurst that characterize the residents. Anyone who is not Italian is seen as an outsider invading the neighborhood (8). The residents have set up a certain way of living that rarely changes. But what can be viewed as an honest, even healthy pride in a neighborhood can easily become racism, which manifests itself in an "us versus them" attitude. As the author puts it in paragraph 10, "Italian Americans in Bensonhurst are notable for their cohesiveness and provinciality; the slightest pressure turns those qualities into prejudice and racism."

3. Bensonhurst was obviously limiting to Torgovnick, who felt that if she stayed she would not get the education and lifestyle she wanted. Her escape, however, is obviously not complete because, throughout the essay, there is a sense that her past is always with her. Her roots, she writes in paragraph 18, have a both "choking and nutritive power." She has put some physical distance between herself and Bensonhurst, but her family connections keep her tied to Brooklyn, as do meetings with other "expatriates," such as the fellow professors with whom she has dinner (19-23). In paragraphs 16 through 18, she notes that she lives much differently in her large Durham home than she did in Brooklyn, but that this "superior" way of living is only a superficial contrast. The simple fact that she has written such a passionate and deeply felt essay bears testimony to the continuing strength of her ties to Bensonhurst.

4. Her roots both sustain her and make her feel trapped. They sustain her because, regardless of how she feels, her past in Bensonhurst played an important role in her intellectual and emotional development, if only to show her what she did not want in life. They choke her, however, because they remind her of how easily her life could have been held back had she stayed there and chosen not to get out by going to college and graduate school, marrying, and moving out of state.

5. She seems to be pointing to the irony that these three highly educated professors all came from a place they recall as inferior and anti-intellectual. The fact that these three escaped from Bensonhurst comforts the author, to the extent that they almost seem like triumphant survivors who share a past they would rather not admit.

6. The final anecdote is a fitting conclusion because, in the scene, the author defies her neighborhood by doing what a woman is not supposed to do. She entered an inner sanctum for the male residents of the neighborhood and broke the traditional taboos and patterns, just as she had done repeatedly throughout her life there.

Writing Topics (p. 499)

1. This might prove to be a difficult organizational project for students, who will probably tell a story about their neighborhoods or value systems and then jump to comment on it. These comments may tend to generalize and moralize. Ask students to set the scene completely by finding the best illustrative anecdote and then, moving from past memory to present commentary, to make a reasoned statement about how that incident influenced them for better or worse.

2. This is the kind of topic that will bring deep emotions to the surface. Students should be sensitive to their own biases and judgments, as well as those of other students. In discussing mixed marriages, students might relate personal experiences to support or argue against this type of relationship.

Immigrants

Pat Mora

Questions for Study and Discussion (p. 502)

1. On the surface, being American means eating certain foods such as hot dogs and apple pie (2), having certain names and physical characteristics (3-5), playing with dolls and footballs (4-6), and using English (7-8). The author seems to be working, sarcastically, on specific stereotypes; students may or may not see the biting, even sad, irony. Interestingly, she does not include "American" feelings, such as patriotism, or attitudes, including pride or a work ethic.

2. By leaving "american" uncapitalized as the immigrant parents whisper the word, the poet suggests that the parents, trying desperately to secure their children's assimilation, don't have the luxury of investing "America" with any particular romance or high-flown idealism. In this context, the word appears as an adjective, which they hope to attach to their children by dint of urgent repetition.

3. Speaking English in public demonstrates that the immigrants are being assimilated into the American mainstream. Whispering their native language in a "dark bed" suggests a certain furtiveness and shame in not being definitively "American." The speaker uses "thick English" to describe English spoken with a foreign accent.

4. Talking at night, the parents fear that their children will not be completely accepted as Americans and that they will remain second-class, less privileged citizens.

5. "They" indicates mainstream society. It may mean the children's

fellow students at school or the playground, or the adults in the family's neighborhood; in any case, the vagueness is appropriate in this context.

6. The poet's irony makes it difficult to say definitively what she thinks about assimilation. Lines 1 to 8 seem to satirize both the parents' desperation and the bland American stereotypes they want their children to emulate. However, their parental concern and vulnerability are portrayed sympathetically in the poem's second half. It is probably safe to say that the poet is not "for" conformity, but the poem shows her compassion for those feeling its pressure.

Writing Topics (p. 502)

1. The responses will depend on whether students consider themselves insiders or outsiders in American culture; responses may also vary according to different regions of the country. Family stories of new immigrants attempting to fit into American society while keeping their heritage will enrich student essays. Students might consider whether they are proud of or embarrassed by their immigrant grandparents or parents, for instance. They might compare the feelings in this poem about assimilation and cultural unity and diversity with those of Edite Cunha ("Talking in the New Land," p. 478) or Ji-Yeon Mary Yuhfill ("Let's Tell the Story of All America's Cultures," p. 348).

2. This is a chance for students to talk with their relatives and write up their family lore. They might focus on the expectations of America for immigrants and how those expectations were matched, or not, by reality. As an exercise, then, this assignment can allow students to gather material from oral interviews or challenge them to turn real-life events into a fictionalized account. Students might also draw on immigrant stories that they have seen in the movies or on television.

7 / Contemporary Issues

The Human Cost of an Illiterate Society

Jonathan Kozol

Questions for Study and Discussion (p. 512)

1. Kozol sets a tone of urgency by letting the reader speculate on the dangers an illiterate faces everyday in every aspect of life.

2. Kozol recounts daily situations requiring an ability to read that are faced by all illiterates. He is convincing when he shows that all aspects of daily life demand an ability to read. For example, he tells of one illiterate

103

who was stranded after his car broke down because he could not tell the police where he was.

3. Kozol implies that a lack of wealth and privilege, as well as prejudice, contributes to illiteracy.

4. According to Kozol, an illiterate society is unable to uphold and defend democracy and, in a society dependent upon the written word, illiterates are at the mercy of those who are literate.

5. Kozol makes a rational appeal using convincing examples of the many ways illiterates are at a disadvantage in daily social situations. However, some students may argue that the problem is not as extreme for all illiterates.

6. Kozol does not give illiterates credit for remembering and verbalizing. Illiteracy is not linked to IQ in all cases. For example, renting an apartment should not be difficult for an intelligent person, whether he can read and write or not. Most people know what the rent will be long before they sign the lease.

7. Throughout the essay Kozol provides examples that portray illiterates as defenseless, economically deprived, disenfranchised, and unable to participate in the system.

Writing Topics (p. 512)

1. As a prewriting activity you may encourage students to research the works of PLUS--Project Literacy U.S. The students may contact different chapters of PLUS that deal with different areas of the nation or their state to discern where the problem areas are and if the solution to illiteracy is the same in these problem areas as in the less afflicted areas.

2. This is a good assignment to make the students aware of the problem in "their" world. It is very easy to recognize that a problem exists, but it is not so easy to realize that it exists so close to home. Firsthand accounts from professors or students that illiteracy occurs on college campuses could enlighten some students.

Abortion Is Too Complex to Feel All One Way About

Anna Quindlen

Questions for Study and Discussion (p. 515)

1. The stories Quindlen tells at the beginning of her essay are effective because they immediately set up for the reader the limits and nature of Quindlen's dilemma in the emotional, compassionate tone she will use throughout her essay.

2. Quindlen's beliefs that "it is the right thing in some times and places," "the issue of abortion is difficult for all thoughtful people," and "legally I want always to have that right" have in common a concern for the men and women who face the decision to have an abortion. Her uncertainty over whether "a woman's right to choose [is] absolute," and her doubt that the unborn child is "a little blob of formless protoplasm," reflect her awareness of and compassion for the unborn child.

3. Since experiencing pregnancy and childbirth, Quindlen is no longer certain that a woman has the moral right to abort a pregnancy under any and all circumstances.

4. Some students will argue that Quindlen, who has wealth and a supportive mate, is not representative of many women facing abortion. Even though Quindlen makes that point herself, her position may still strike some readers as luxurious. On the other hand, some students may argue that it is precisely and only those who have been pregnant who can authentically address the issue of abortion.

5. Quindlen groups herself with the "thoughtful," those for whom there are no easy answers or absolutes in the question of abortion. She reveals a marked animosity and disdain for the antiabortionists, whom she describes as "smug and sometimes violent" and fanatical in nature. Quindlen is easier on the supporters of abortion rights (among whom she still counts herself), although she does chastise them for taking a "monolithic position" against the antiabortionists.

6. Quindlen's audience, readers of the New York Times, are educated, sophisticated, and liberal. She risks offending a readership that she must assume will tend to be pro-choice. However, she has strong feelings on the subject and has developed insights that will possibly de-polarize the abortion debate, a "closet" wish for many "thoughtful" people. Quindlen is counting on the fact that her audience will listen to her argument since she has established liberal credentials of her own.

<u>Writing Topics (p. 516)</u>

1. Before students begin work on this assignment it may be helpful to analyze with them examples of letters written to the editorial page of a local newspaper. Consider each in terms of its construction as an argument, noting especially the selection and organization of supporting evidence. You can also examine other features related to successful arguments as they are outlined under the following headings in the glossary: Argument, Deduction, Induction, Logical Fallacies, and Persuasion. After reviewing these concepts and applying them to sample letters, students may be better equipped to write a rebuttal to an article dealing with a controversial social issue.

2. The easiest way to approach this assignment would be to have the students write their essay with an epilogue discussing the ease or difficulty

of writing their emotional essays. You may want to remind students that tone and diction will be very important for the body of the essay. Students may review the glossary entries at the back of the book for tone and diction. The epilogues may be interesting to share with the class when the assignment is done.

A Brother's Murder

Brent Staples

Questions for Study and Discussion (p. 519)

   1. This opening is effective because it is so immediate and direct. There is nothing to distract from the central message that Blake had been brutally murdered. The opening sentence is most upsetting because of its universality: Most people have experienced terrible news from an unexpected phone call. The first paragraph sets the tone for the rest of the essay because the paragraphs that follow are similarly sad, mournful, and direct, even blunt.

   2. Staples first encountered mortality growing up in the gritty city of Chester. A series of attempted and actual murders of those close to him-- acquaintances, friends, and relatives--began when he was fourteen years old. They happened so frequently and rapidly that "the summers blur" (2). What is unusual about these violent encounters is that all of them were so casual: The victims who survived bragged about their attacks, and most of the murders began with a simple misunderstanding, such as a fight over a game of pool.

   3. Staples uses these incidents to draw a parallel between the war in Vietnam and the wars taking place on city streets. He also draws a closer link: The soldiers and the young men in the neighborhood act the same way. Both wear their manhood on their sleeves and are interested in parading their lack of fear. "Killing is only machismo taken to the extreme" (3) illustrates Staples's point that young men in the ghetto are often driven to prove their manhood however they can. Killing becomes the most direct and dramatic way of doing so.

   4. Staples is educated, well-to-do, and successful. He has escaped Chester and now lives on quiet street, has worked as a teacher and journalist, and is climbing the professional and social ranks (4). Blake is stuck in a housing project, is involved with drugs, uses a shotgun, and thinks himself immortal. There is a "dangerous light" in his eyes (6). In paragraphs 6 and 7, the fear and foreboding Staples feels for his brother are evident. Staples sees the inevitable result of Blake's life, but his younger brother does not.

106

5. Staples feels that he should have done more to help his brother and prevent his death. Instead of suggesting that Blake leave his home in Roanoke, for instance, perhaps Staples believes he should have taken him away himself. The disturbing, recurrent dream Staples has indicates that he blames himself for Blake's death.

Writing Topics (p. 519)

1. Responses will vary widely according to the social and racial background of students. Students with strong points of view should be encouraged to see another side of this situation. Some students may write naive, theoretical essays; ask them to test their theories with stories taken from tabloid television shows and newspapers, as well as their own experiences.
2. "Machismo" can mean assorted things to students of diverse cultural and ethnic backgrounds. These variations should be directly discussed with respect to positive and negative perceptions and effects.

Why Worry About the Animals?

Jean Bethke Elshtain

Questions for Study and Discussion (p. 529)

1. The list tends to shock and disgust the reader. This type of introduction lets the reader know that an assault on this type of activity will follow in the rest of the essay. The stark brutality of these sentences is effective because the reader is immediately drawn into the subject matter.
2. The new activists tend to be more aggressive, engaging in civil disobedience that places a higher value on action than preaching. This is due to a more positive view of animals: They have rights, must be protected and liberated, and may even be considered equals. The proliferation of peace and justice issues may have contributed to the growth of the new breed of animal-rights activists who are concerned with planetary conservation and similar environmental issues. The older animal enthusiasts were traditionally motivated by charitable and sentimental emotions.
3. Elshtain makes her objections known in paragraphs 16 to 20. She objects to the dark conditions in which veal calves are kept, the polluted habitats of pandas, and the threat posed to wild animals such as elephants by poachers. She also protests against using animals, including greyhounds, whales, and dolphins, for entertainment, and using monkeys for experiments, especially those dealing with war and radiation.
4. The LD50 test checks the toxicity of household products like floor

wax and lipstick. The use of this test is objectionable because animals are injected with toxic substances for the sole purpose of making them sick. Only when one-half of the animals tested die are the tests discontinued. Neither painkillers nor anesthesia are used. Ironically, these tests are unreliable and therefore largely useless.

5. The bumper sticker indicates what some people are willing to give up and suggests how important guns are to them, as well as how powerful the National Rifle Association lobby can be. Too much of the point of the example is left unclear, however: Disturbing issues suggested about women and pets are left unresolved.

6. Most people would probably agree with this list. The author respects her readers and thereby probably gains their support for her argument. In paragraph 14, she similarly praises well-intentioned people and in paragraph 40 she criticizes the extremism to which most people would object. This strategy also enlists the readers' sympathies.

7. As the author puts it in paragraph 39, resistance to making human changes is supported by "old habits, bad science, unreflective cruelty, profit, and, in some cases, a genuine fear that animal-welfare groups want to stop all research dead in its tracks."

8. The similarity between animals and humans is cited by advocates as a justification for animal experimentation, because it means that experimental findings will be applicable to human beings. The irony is that if animals were truly seen as "like" human beings, sympathy and conscience would prevent performing experiments on them that would not be performed on humans.

9. Elshtain tells the reader her positions in paragraphs 40 to 45. She does not believe that animal experiments necessarily end human suffering or that performing experiments on animals is necessary for curing human diseases such as AIDS. Most animal experiments, she contends, are not linked to alleviating human suffering anyway. Also, animal experiments are not consistent with the new view of the world and nature, which sees the planet as something to be enjoyed and preserved instead of exploited. Her statement that she had polio is important because it bolsters her credibility by showing that she has a powerful reason to support effective medical research.

10. This firsthand account of animal cruelty serves to conclude the essay vividly and complements the introduction: The anecdote reminds the reader of the examples in the opening paragraphs and thus contributes to the essay's persuasiveness and unity. It also effectively demonstrates one final time how the author's heart and mind are involved in this issue.

1. Students might consider the four points separately, arguing the pros and cons of each. They should then try to weigh the sum total of the argument, offering counterexamples and countervailing evidence. In the third position Elshtain offers, she mentions human cases that should be debated item by item. Perhaps students can come up with one such item and follow the author's suggestion to debate by drawing up a case study from recent newspaper accounts or classic textbook examples. Likewise, they might take the suggestion of the second position and discuss whether humans should be subjects of medical experimentation if they choose to be, relating this especially to the current situation concerning the search for a cure to AIDS.

2. A debate between a vegetarian and a non-vegetarian would make an interesting paper and challenge students to use Socratic dialogue as a way of working out their opinions and tracking opposing sides of an issue. They might also think about whether being both a meat-eater and an animal-rights advocate is an impossible position, or whether eating meat is an inconsequential compromise.

3. Library research on this topic will afford interested students the opportunity to join English with science, subjects not normally linked directly in schoolwork. They can discuss whether the relative merits of stricter monitoring are worth the cost, too.

What Is the Truth About Global Warming?

Robert James Bidinotto

Questions for Study and Discussion (p. 535)

1. The greenhouse effect is described by Bidinotto in the following way in paragraph 5: When sunlight warms the earth, there are certain gases in the lower atmosphere that act like the glass in a greenhouse. These gases, found primarily in water vapors including carbon dioxide, methane, and chlorofluorocarbons, make our planet warmer and in the process make life possible. If these gases become too abundant, they could trap too much heat, which is where the danger arises. The process that could bring about this overabundance of gases is a buildup of greenhouse gases in the atmosphere. This buildup is caused by a combination of natural occurrences (decaying plants, breathing, volcanoes) and man-made problems (chlorofluorocarbons escaping from spray cans, refrigerators, and air conditioners). According to Bidinotto, some scientists are worried, but others feel there is not enough evidence to support the theory.

2. Scientists feel that people play a part in the buildup of greenhouse gases by burning wood and fossil fuels, which can cause an excess of carbon dioxide. Also, more methane has been produced because of the increase in cattle raising and uses of natural gases. The main culprit seems to be chlorofluorocarbons, which escape from man-made products such as plastic foam, solvents, spray cans, and refrigerators.

3. Bidinotto quotes Frederick in paragraph 16 as saying, "You would experience a much greater increase in biologically damaging ultraviolet radiation if you moved from New York City to Atlanta than you would with the ozone depletion that we estimate will occur over the next 30 years." Bidinotto leaves the quote unexplained and we do not find out why Frederick believes this is so.

4. Scientists agree that if greenhouse gases increase and all other factors remain the same that the earth will warm up; however, they also agree that the key is "to what extent other factors remain the same" (19). Scientists appear skeptical about the greenhouse effect because there are still many things about climatic forces and how they interact that are not yet understood. Until scientists can understand them, the greenhouse effect remains a theory.

5. El Niño was a current in the tropical Pacific that caused great changes in atmospheric temperature during the 1980s. After the El Niño incident, scientists included ocean currents in climate simulations, which seemed to diminish the likelihood that parts of the Antarctic would warm.

6. Computer models that try to determine the future of the greenhouse effect are problematic because the computer, according to Bidinotto, "is no more reliable than its input, and poorly understood oceanic, atmospheric and continental processes are only crudely represented even in the best GCMs" (27).

Clouds, which cover 60 percent of the planet at any given time, cannot only trap heat radiating from the surface, but they also reflect sunlight back into space. Once scientists factored these cloud patterns into their computer models, the global-warming projections were cut in half.

7. Politicians have jumped on the global-warming bandwagon, maintaining that "even if the theory is wrong, [they] will be doing the right thing in terms of economic and environmental policy" (32). It has become fashionable for politicians to be concerned about environmental problems. Bidinotto, however, says that scientists are concerned because the evidence is still inconclusive and should not be used for "political advocacy" (33).

8. Bidinotto tries his best to answer the question posed in the title with the information available to him. He is successful because he explores different views and theories involved in the search for the truth about global warming. He ends the essay by saying that more research is needed before we are able to understand the greenhouse effect.

1. Students may wish to take the suggested measures in paragraph 30 and apply them to their own lives to see how hard or easy it would be to attempt to make them a part of their routine. They may also try to come up with their own solutions, but should take into account whether they are realistic measures. Discussion may include the pros and cons of banning the use of chlorofluorocarbons and how such a ban would affect the general population.

2. An open discussion about what each student knows or believes to be true about global warming may be helpful in this situation. Comparing true statements to statements based largely on hearsay may prove that jumping to conclusions without facts is not they way to deal with problems in the environment. Students may wish to take each of the institutions listed in the question and explore the differences and similarities in the ways they deal with global warming.

3. Students may wish simply to argue about the statement itself, or they could imagine a situation where a "scary scenario" causes more harm because people act upon it in a drastic way without knowing the facts.

Fear in a Handful of Numbers

Dennis Overbye

Questions for Study and Discussion (p. 540)

1. This expression is generally intended to mean that we cannot change the everyday weather. However, Overbye suggests that we do in fact affect the weather by virtue of our carelessness.

2. Overbye's audience, the readers of Time magazine, is the lay public, albeit an educated, sophisticated one. The cowboy and Indian analogy is particularly fitting because it conjures an image of eternal struggle in the uniquely "true grit" American style.

3. In paragraph 3, Overbye asks four questions that he answers almost immediately by insisting that we take action to save our earth. His notion of "pretending" until a "real" commitment is made seems reasonable if you believe, as cognitive therapists do, that thought precedes action. Thus we can work to change our thoughts and, as a result, change our actions.

4. Pollution kills our habitat, without which we will eventually die.

5. Overbye uses the following metaphors: "Los Angelenos whipping their sunny basin into a brown blur on the way to work every morning" (1); "nature was metaphorically transformed. It became dead meat" (4); "victory ovor nature is a kind of suicide" (6); "what we have now is a sort of

biological equivalent to a black hole" (6). Each of these metaphors helps clarify the author's ideas by putting them in terms the reader will understand. The metaphors have also been chosen to jolt the reader with a brutality that insists we don't have decades in which to ponder the fine points of the argument.

6. Although science is a "cowboy" achievement, it actually favors the "Indian" view of nature as alive.

7. For Overbye, numbers can help us "read" the progress of our self-destruction. Overbye suggests that we need more science to calculate the hazards we are creating and make us aware of the problems we face. Overbye is therefore offering science, not as progress, but as a picture of reality. Thus he resolves the seeming contradiction in suggesting that science step forward to solve the problems of too rapid progress.

8. "Payment" for our prosperity and taking what we want will be the courage to make do with less as a means of persuading the rest of the world to do likewise.

9. Rather than argue for the typical conservation measures for which environmentalists plead, Overbye suggests that we change our frame of mind, that we "pretend."

Writing Topics (p. 541)

1. Students may discuss Overbye's arguments with a professor of environmental studies to get a second opinion on what options, if any, are feasible in counteracting the greenhouse effect. By researching feasible options students can answer for themselves who should be approached to eliminate the effects and what success can be expected.

2. As a prewriting activity you may find it helpful to discuss the writer's purpose and tone in each of these essays. For example, Bidinotto questions the lack of data on global warming and therefore the very basis for taking particular action with respect to possible courses of action in combating it. His tone is questioning and cautious. Overbye, on the other hand, is optimistic in his belief that we are fortunate to have the technology to solve our environmental problems. Such a discussion will help students focus on the differences between the two writers as well as develop a position of their own on this question.

Active and Passive Euthanasia

James Rachels

Questions for Study and Discussion (p. 547)

1. Rachels's thesis is that there is no meaningful moral distinction between active euthanasia--killing terminally ill or injured patients--and

112

passive euthanasia--letting them die of their disabilities (1). Nowhere in the essay does he actually support euthanasia of either kind, and the sordid example he chooses to give in paragraphs 10 to 12 hints that he may actually be against euthanasia, since it introduces an otherwise gratuitously ugly note into his discussion.

2. To supplement the answer to question 1 above, we would add that the most substantial difference Rachels discusses is that passive euthanasia may often permit a much more prolonged and painful death than would active euthanasia (3-4), so that active euthanasia may actually be the more humane. However, active euthanasia is against the law (19) and against the American Medical Association's ethical standards (1), and people in general consider it less ethical.

3. The example of the child with Down's syndrome is not directly relevant to the issue because, as Rachels points out in paragraph 6, an operation that is "not prohibitively difficult" would save the baby's life. Rather, the parents have decided that living with Down's syndrome would be worse for their child (or for them) than if the child died, and so they permit the child to die from an unrelated and remediable defect. (See S. I. Hayakawa, "Our Son Mark," p. 105, for what might have happened had the child been saved.) Rachels includes this example partly to make more clear by negation what passive euthanasia is and partly to include the poignant image of a tiny baby dying in needlessly prolonged pain.

4. The Smith-Jones case tests Rachels's claim that there is no moral difference between killing people and letting them die, and prepares for his discussion in paragraph 15 of why so many think there _is_ a moral difference. Creating a hypothetical example allows Rachels to determine fully the specific points of the comparison he wants to make; in real life, exactly parallel situations like the Smith-Jones case rarely occur. However, the example's strength is also its weakness, as some readers may find it contrived and unconvincing.

5. Rachels wrote his article to convince doctors in general, and those who write the American Medical Association's ethical pronouncements in particular, that they should reconsider the view that active euthanasia is "contrary to that for which the medical profession stands," whereas passive euthanasia is left to "the patient and/or his immediate family" to decide (1). His expected readers are doctors, as we know partly from the essay's source (the New England Journal of Medicine) and partly from the last sentence of paragraph 1. But obviously the article is understandable by and relevant to a general audience.

Writing Topics (p. 548)

1. Since the law and the American Medical Association do permit passive euthanasia in some instances, this is not a wholly hypothetical

question, but it is probably a question that few students have thought about--at least until they read Rachels's essay. Euthanasia asked for by the patient is tantamount to suicide, so students may wish to approach this assignment from the perspective of the moral implications for someone choosing to die and for someone deciding to let someone else die. The distinctions they see, if any, between these two types of action may reveal something about their attitudes toward active versus passive euthanasia.

2. Sources for research can be found in the library under the heading, Euthanasia.

3. This question moves from the issue of euthanasia to a far broader question, one that can be examined from many points of view and using many cases in point--most obviously the "Noble Experiment" of Prohibition. In the broadest sense, however, the purpose of law is to enforce certain moral and ethical rules that grow out of a society's needs and values. To make an act a crime, for example, is nothing if not a legislated moral judgment. The tension between law and morality is greatest, we think, when an act is somehow classified as a crime when much or even most of a society does not believe that act to be immoral or unethical.

How Far She Went

Mary Hood

<u>Questions for Study and Discussion (p. 555)</u>

1. Their relationship is filled with anger and misunderstanding. The difference in their ages makes it difficult for each of them to accept the other's personality. This generation gap makes it virtually impossible for the two to communicate in any way. They are constantly arguing and disagreeing, slamming doors in the process.

2. The father and Sylvie (the granddaughter's mother) were married quickly and had their daughter shortly afterwards. Sylvie died quite young and the father then gave his daughter to his wife's mother. We find out that the father does not want his daughter when he sends word that she should cash in her plane ticket to stay at their grandmother's and buy some school clothes. With her mother dead and her father not interested in her, the granddaughter is forced to stay with her grandmother.

3. The relationship between the grandmother and her daughter, Sylvie, was similar to that between the grandmother and her granddaughter. It seems that the daughter and granddaughter are similar and that the grandmother is going through the same things she went through with her daughter.

4. The dog is described as the one thing the grandmother can count on.

114

The author's description of their relationship is important because later in the story the grandmother will sacrifice the dog's life to save the life of her granddaughter.

5. The grandmother realizes that the motorcyclists only want sex from the young girl. The young girl does not see this and only looks at them as an adventure through which she can get back at her grandmother in some way.

6. The blood ties between the two grow strong because they have gone through a life and death situation together where the grandmother showed love to the granddaughter, a love that the granddaughter never really experienced before. By the end of the story they have a newfound respect and admiration for each other, hence the "ma'am" references. They seem to be on their way to a better understanding of each other.

7. The young girl's mother, Sylvie, is the only character with a name because all of the situations that make up the story stem from her life and how she lived it. For example, the granddaughter could be anyone who has gone through the situation where one parent dies and the other does not want the burden of raising the child.

8. Her style is very descriptive: picturesque scenes, illustrative anecdotes, vivid dialogue, clear images. These qualities enhance her skill as a storyteller because readers can easily visualize the story as it unfolds before their eyes, as if they were watching a film.

Writing Topics (p. 556)

1. Students may wish to discuss situation in their own lives that in some way relate to the story. Such a situation may be one in which someone showed love and concern for them when previous tensions existed. The situation can be between friends, the student and a parent, or siblings, if students choose to be personal. Students may also choose to distance themselves from a difficult set of circumstances by fictionalizing an event taken from life.

2. Students should be encouraged to examine the elements of fiction-- plot, character, conflict, resolution, and so on--in discussing Hood's skills as a writer.

The Declaration of Independence

Thomas Jefferson

<u>Questions for Study and Discussion (p. 562)</u>

1. The purpose of government, according to the Declaration, is to secure "certain unalienable Rights," among them "Life, Liberty and the pursuit of Happiness" (2). These are of course individual rights, and governments also exist to serve other purposes--the adjudication of disputes, for example, and the protection of private property--that do not quite fit the Declaration's formulation. Presumably Jefferson did not feel the need to tell his readers what they already knew and what does not, after all, have much to do with the reasons for revolt against England.

2. At the end of paragraph 2 Jefferson states that "the history of the present King of Great Britain is a history of repeated injuries and usurpations, all having in direct object the establishment of an absolute Tyranny over these States." Jefferson then lists the specific charges against the king in paragraphs 3 through 29.

3. The Declaration offers the argument in paragraph 2 that when a government is despotic it should be abolished and a new one established. The argument is based on the following premises: (a) "all men are created equal"; (b) "they are endowed by their Creator with certain unalienable Rights"; (c) "Governments are instituted" to secure these unalienable rights; and (d) people have a right and a duty to throw off a despotic government. Once these assumptions are accepted, the rest of Jefferson's argument follows logically.

4. In paragraph 31 Jefferson reviews the ways in which the colonies attempted to make the British government aware of their problems.

5. Having established a sound logical argument, Jefferson uses emotionally charged language to call forth feelings of patriotism among the colonists. Examples of Jefferson's emotionally charged language include <u>wholesome</u> (3), <u>refused</u> (5), <u>inestimable</u> (5), <u>formidable</u> (5), <u>tyrants</u> (5), <u>manly</u> (7), <u>swarms</u> (12), and <u>harass</u> (12).

<u>Writing Topics (p. 562)</u>

2. Students will find that, among other things, a powerful and lengthy condemnation of the slave trade was deleted from Jefferson's first draft. That clause began: "He has waged cruel war against human nature itself, violating its most sacred rights of life and liberty in the persons of a distant

people who never offended him, captivating and carrying them into slavery in another hemisphere, or to incur miserable death in their transportation hither." Since several states benefited economically from slavery and would not support any document attacking that institution, the offending clause was removed--and all thirteen colonies adopted the Declaration.

Civil Disobedience

Henry David Thoreau

Questions for Study and Discussion (p. 580)

1. Thoreau's discussion of the possibilities and limitations of government appears in the first two paragraphs. He sees government, at best, as an expedient, "the mode which the people have chosen to execute their will. . . . Governments show . . . how successfully men can be imposed on, even impose on themselves, for their own advantage." But, he continues, "government is an expedient by which men would fain succeed in letting one another alone; and . . . when it is most expedient, the governed are most let alone by it."

Later in the essay Thoreau also states that governments can impose laws enforced by majority rule, but they cannot impose conscience within individuals, and, ultimately, "it is not desirable to cultivate a respect for the law, so much as for the right" (4).

2. Thoreau was jailed for refusing to pay a poll tax collected by the State. In paragraph 26 he describes why he considered himself free even while in jail: "I could not but smile to see how industriously they locked the door on my meditations, which followed them out again without let or hindrance, and they were really all that was dangerous."

3. People should not obey laws they consider unjust, according to Thoreau, who writes, "The only obligation which I have a right to assume is to do at any time what I think right" (4). The alternative is to surrender the dictates of conscience to the authority of the State or of majority rule, neither of which is ultimately based on justice. Thoreau believes justice to be the product of the individual conscience, and only when individual consciences work together for the right, regardless of expediency or law, can a governing body be considered just. He writes: "Why has every man a conscience, then? I think that we should be men first, and subjects afterwards. . . . It is truly enough said that a corporation has no conscience; but a corporation of conscientious men is a corporation with a conscience" (4).

4. Thoreau is sincere but demanding in his attitude against supporting the State when it participates in activities he finds unjust. His remarks are

aimed mainly at the people of his community and of his state, and are an attempt to awaken them from an unthinking, too-facile allegiance to the State. In that attempt he does not mince words, as the following excerpts illustrate: "Those who, while they disapprove of the character and measures of a government, yield to it their allegiance and support are undoubtedly its most conscientious supporters, and so frequently the most serious obstacles to reform" (14); "How can a man be satisfied to entertain an opinion merely, and enjoy it?" (15); "I do not hesitate to say, that those who call themselves Abolitionists should at once effectually withdraw their support, both in person and property, from the government of Massachusetts, and not wait till they constitute a majority of one, before they suffer the right to prevail through them" (20).

5. Thoreau's purpose is to get others to act as he has, so that the State will be forced to discontinue its activities in support of slavery and the Mexican War. He is not merely trying to rationalize his own behavior since, as is clear throughout the essay, he has little regard for how people respond to his unorthodox behavior: He acts according to his conscience rather than according to the expediency of law or public opinion.

6. Danile Webster serves as an example of those statesmen and legislators who "standing so completely within the institution, never distinctly and nakedly behold it." According to Thoreau, "Webster never goes behind government, and so cannot speak with authority about it. . . . His quality is not wisdom, but prudence. . . . Notwithstanding his special acuteness and ability, he is unable to take a fact out of its merely political relations, and behold it as it lies absolutely to be disposed of by the intellect" (42).

Students' opinions on Thoreau's assessment of Webster may vary, and will likely suggest how they feel about Webster's single-minded devotion to the Constitution.

7. Thoreau uses a variety of techniques to support and document his claims. To give philosophical credence to the positions he maintains he refers to sources such as the Bible, Shakespeare, and other philosophers and poets. He mentions the events that have taken place around him--in his community, in the state, and in the nation--to document his claims about the injustice being done in regard to slavery and the Mexican War. And, finally, he uses his own experiences to support his views about the need for and justness of civil disobedience.

Writing Topics (p. 580)

1. As a prewriting activity designed to provide students with a body of information from which they can shape their essays for this topic, you can ask them to do research into examples of unjust imprisonment in recent history and then have them share the results of their work in class,

discussing the context of Thoreau's statement as it applies to their examples. This type of classroom activity may help students formulate opinions about the validity of Thoreau's statement.

2. As a prewriting discussion for this topic you can ask students to consider Thoreau's statement "The only obligation which I have a right to assume is to do at any time what I think right." Students have probably encountered examples, in their own lives or through the news media, of situations where someone who felt he was doing right was also acting in a way extremely harmful to others or to society. Given such situations, find out how students would reconcile Thoreau's statement with the notion of public good or even public safety. Your discussion may yield some insights into the difficulties of reconciling individual conscience with majority rule.

3. As suggested in writing topic 1 for "Letter from Birmingham Jail" (see p. 120 in this manual), students can also research the works of Mahatma Gandhi and consider how they relate to both Thoreau and King, especially since Gandhi's life falls between these other two.

Declaration of Sentiments and Resolutions

Elizabeth Cady Stanton

Questions for Study and Discussion (p. 586)

1. Stanton no doubt wished to remind her listeners and readers of the moral basis on which our American system of government was established, while at the same time to indicate that in the treatment of women that moral basis was not being upheld.

2. The intent of parody is to burlesque or criticize through humor the content or style of another work. Stanton is not interested in doing this in her treatment of the Declaration of Independence. She is very serious about drawing attention to the principles upon which our government rests, in order that she may point out how women have been excluded from the full benefit of those principles. Her presentation of "self-evident truths" suggests that she believes firmly in the precepts outlined by Thomas Jefferson, and that those precepts provide a moral and civil basis for her fight for women's rights. In short, parody means to undermine the intent of the work it is modeled on, whereas Stanton wishes instead to reinforce the meaning and importance of the Declaration of Independence.

3. In general, the women at the Seneca Falls convention want it recognized that the great precept of Nature--that "man shall pursue his own true and substantial happiness"--applies to men and women equally. A more specific listing of individual demands related to that precept is presented in paragraphs 23 to 35.

4. The "elective franchise" is the right to vote. It is fundamental to Stanton's argument because none of the other issues she mentions can be addressed properly until women are given an elective voice in establishing the conditions under which they are to live. As Stanton states in paragraph 7, "Having deprived [woman] of this first right of a citizen, the elective franchise, thereby leaving her without representation in the halls of legislation, [man] has oppressed her on all sides."

5. Stanton's statement refers to the fact that once married, a woman's rights became secondary to those of her husband, leaving her no legal recourse should she wish to assert her rights independent of her husband's will.

6. Since, in paragraph 3, Stanton states that "the history of mankind is a history of repeated injuries and usurpations on the part of man toward woman, having in direct object the establishment of an absolute tyranny over her," the repeated references to "He" in the list of abuses that follows indicate men, in general, through the history of mankind.

The rhetorical effect of listing the abuses as she has, and beginning each with "He," is an acute sense of emphasis, and an escalating awareness of the extent to which men have tyrannized women. There is also the reminder of the similar use of "He" in reference to King George in the Declaration of Independence, reinforcing the degree of tyranny.

7. As the final resolution in paragraph 35 suggests, Stanton's declaration is aimed at both men and women.

8. If Stanton had concluded her declaration at paragraph 20, it would only have provided a list of grievances and, therefore, created only a sense of destructive action without an accompanying sense of constructive counteraction. The list of resolutions provides a concrete description of exactly how women wish to change the abusive conditions outlined in paragraphs 4 to 18.

9. Students' responses to this question may vary. We see no such indicators of "feminine" writing.

Writing Topics (p. 586)

1. As a prewriting activity for this topic, it may be interesting to compare Stanton's declaration with the founding doctrine or constitution of a currently active women's organization like NOW (the National Organization for Women). Such a comparison should help students respond to the questions of what issues still need to be addressed and what new complaints have been voiced in the last twenty years. A look at the debate surrounding attempts at passing the Equal Rights Amendment may also provide useful information in this regard.

2. In looking at Jefferson's document, students can substitute "women" for all the references to the American colonists and "men" for all the

references to England or King George, to see what effect it has on their reading of the Declaration, and how the Declaration would then compare to Stanton's document. They may be surprised at how conveniently the substitutions can be made, and might therefore be able to draw conclusions about Stanton's use of the Declaration of Independence as the model for her own Declaration of Sentiments and Resolutions.

A Woman's Fight

Pretty Shield

Questions for Study and Discussion (p. 590)

1. The older woman was probably proud of--and amused by--the young girl's naive bravery. This story portends Strikes-two's courage, which had a great, life-or-death impact on the village. Pretty Shield's little effort points to Strikes-two's bravery, which was on a larger, more important scale.

2. Pretty Shield is proud of the woman's effort. She both foreshadowed the event with her own actions and, more pertinently, now acts as the storyteller who keeps the incident alive in the minds of her listeners and readers.

3. To be "sent out as a wolf" meant to act as a lookout: to see what was around without being seen.

4. In paragraph 8, Pretty Shield indicates that she was the witness to this event and that she is reliable because she saw it firsthand.

5. The Lacota feared Strikes-two because of her boldness and powers as a medicine woman (12). The Crow men are unwilling to tell of her success because it was a woman who secured the victory, thus ensuring the safety of the village. Apparently, Crow men denigrated women; they must have considered them the weaker sex and in need of protection. The men resented that it was a woman who did the protecting in this case.

6. Pretty Shield is sharing her pride. She is not simply telling a story, but bearing testimony to the courage of this medicine woman by attesting to her actions in battle.

7. Crow men probably assigned women traditional female roles: cooking, cleaning, raising the children. They assigned themselves traditional male roles: hunting, fighting, and making decisions about the village.

Writing Topics (p. 590)

1. Women often are said to engage in "cat fighting": mean and nasty battles that are fought on a small or petty scale. Men are supposed to fight epic battles that prove their manhood. Tough women are considered

unfeminine Amazons who threaten male sexuality. Men might feel demeaned by such women, so they mock them. Students should discuss the double standard that is at work and try to identify events in which men and women broke gender types when fighting or being protected.

2. As a prewriting exercise, students can list what characteristics they think heroes and heroines exhibit in theory. Then, after providing first-person testimony to a heroic act as Pretty Shield did, they can consider how this hero or heroine matched their expectations. They can then rework their definition, which will help them think about and edit their own writing.

3. The question can be raised about whether students should discuss heroism in general or separate the topic into female and male categories. The matter of a collective consciousness or heritage can also be broached: If there are many types of people in a society, should they all contribute a hero to the collective heritage? Which segments of American society are not now represented by heroes?

Letter from Birmingham Jail

Martin Luther King, Jr.

Questions for Study and Discussion (p. 604)

1. King wrote the letter in response to a statement by fellow clergymen that his activities were "unwise and untimely." King was in Birmingham at the request of the Alabama Christian Movement for Human Rights; he led nonviolent demonstrations--sit-ins and marches--against racism and segregation and was arrested for these efforts as an "outside agitator."

2. King believed that he stood in the middle, between the forces of complacency and acceptance and those of bitterness and violence. His middle ground consisted of active nonviolent efforts to oppose and end segregation.

3. King sees the contemporary church as too often "an archdefender of the status quo" (38), whereas the early church acted as a "thermostat that transformed the mores of society" (37).

4. The objection that he was an "outsider" did not apply because King had been invited to Birmingham, because injustice was there, and because no citizen of America can be an "outsider" within its boundaries.

In response to the objection concerning direct action and demonstrations, King replies that these activities are meant to oppose injustice and violence, not initiate them. He describes in detail the orderly process of such activities.

To the charge of "untimeliness" he quotes a distinguished jurist: "Justice too long delayed is justice denied."

King responds to the anxiety that he and his organization are breaking laws by quoting Augustine's "an unjust law is no law at all."

He demonstrates the illogic of the charge that peaceful action precipitates violence; he identifies Christ, Amos, and St. Paul as fellow extremists; and he protests the commendations of the Birmingham police's public behavior by providing examples of their private brutality.

5. King calls upon the clergy to respond in an active, aggressive way to alleviate racism and end segregation. He wishes them to honor the basic tenets of Christianity and the fundamentals of the Constitution and the Declaration of Independence.

6. King views racism and segregation as forms of spiritual violence. He recommends that people oppose this violence by peacefully resisting oppression, demonstrating against it with direct action in the form of sit-ins and marches. He responds to the praise of the Birmingham police by revealing their brutal private behavior and by condemning their purpose, the preservation of "the evil system of segregation."

7. King's audience is the general public, both white and African-American, who need to be informed of the intents and purposes of the nonviolent movement. Though sorely tried, King avoids anger, bitterness, or harangue. He pays careful attention to the potential prejudices and objections of his audience and consistently maintains a reasonable, even gentlemanly, tone.

Writing Topics (p. 605)

1. In preparation for this assignment students may also wish to seek out information on the works and writings of India's Mahatma Gandhi to see what applications they can find in his actions and ideas of principles taken from Thoreau. They can then compare Gandhi's writings on nonviolent resistance to Martin Luther King Jr.'s "Letter from Birmingham Jail," to see if the two men have interpreted Thoreau's principle of civil disobedience in the same manner.

2. As a prewriting activity for this topic you can discuss nonviolent resistance and its alternatives in connection with a current battle being waged to bring about social or legal change. The recent activities of anti-abortion advocates can serve as a good focus for such a discussion, since these advocates represent a wide range of opinions about how to attack the abortion issue. Having students do a bit of research on the matter before they come to class may generate more specific information about the tactics proposed by the various anti-abortion groups, and may in turn provide students with a concrete base of information from which to consider the issue of nonviolent resistance in light of its alternatives.

The Unknown Citizen

W. H. Auden

<u>Questions for Study and Discussion (p. 607)</u>

1. The poem is ironic, as is revealed, for example, by the exaggerated materialism of lines 18 to 21, the doctrinaire complacency of lines 22 to 24, and the joke in line 27--nobody, not even the most obtuse statistician, would say such things in public. The views are those of the State (which erected the monument on which the poem is said to be inscribed), which here has the voice and soul of the insensitive paper-pushers and statisticians of contemporary bureaucracy.

2. Whatever is inscribed on a public monument usually reflects not only the State's view but also majority public opinion, so Auden is able to satirize not only the bureaucratic outlook but also the materialistic values of a large segment of contemporary society. The title suggests that just as the military virtues of bravery and self-sacrifice are celebrated through the Unknown Soldier, likewise the peacetime "virtues" of political docility and consumption of goods can be embodied in the Unknown Citizen.

3. We are given some objective information about the Citizen: where he worked, for example, and that he paid his dues, reacted normally to advertisements, carried a Health-card, used the installment plan, owned basic appliances, was married, and raised five children. However, the poem omits all mention of the Citizen's feelings and aspirations, except to dismiss the subject in the last two lines; what the State has not "heard" and cannot quantify is unimportant. Since the poem is ironic, however, we can conclude almost by definition that Auden's attitudes and values are the opposite of the State's.

4. Since the Citizen's identification number is given he is not really unknown, but the inscription strips away his individuality and humanity. (Alert students may notice the hidden rhyme <u>378/State</u>.)

5. Through his use of capital letters, Auden is implying that the state has reified abstractions--and at the same time, by capitalizing such mundane expressions as "Instalment Plan," he is mocking that tendency.

6. Auden must have intended his readers to join him in his dislike of bureaucracy, and also no doubt in his contempt for materialism. The bland effrontery of the last two lines would surely anger most readers, and the suggestion that a few household appliances are "everything necessary to the Modern Man" (20) is so reductive as to compel opposition.

<u>Writing Topics (p. 607)</u>

1. Many students will enjoy updating Auden's satire of the materialistic, conformist citizen and substituting contemporary references. This

assignment also provides the opportunity for a discussion of generalizations and stereotypes.

2. This activity, a variant on the ever-popular assignment to "write your own obituary," asks students to consider what they would be most proud to have achieved. Also, since they are writing of themselves in the third person, they are required to objectify themselves, choosing an appropriate tone and selecting details that would be of general public interest.

3. The information the government collects directly through census, tax, draft, and medical forms is often essential for planning and funding public programs. But many worry that such information may be misused by government or improperly leaked to private inquirers. In preparation for this assignment, therefore, you can discuss with students exactly what information the government has about them, what constructive purposes that information might serve, and what harm might be done by its improper use. You can also examine how the growth in electronic information recording and storage has facilitiated the government's capacity to collect such data, and to what ultimate effect.

The Lottery

Shirley Jackson

Questions for Study and Discussion (p. 616)

1. The first hint that there is something sinister about the lottery occurs in paragraph 43 when Tessie yells out nervously that her husband did not have enough time to draw. The family is not happy about being the chosen one. If readers remember the children making piles of stones, they may guess what the lottery is. By paragraph 75, the reader is sure that Tessie will be stoned.

2. Jackson uses matter-of-fact description to present "normality." She describes a day that is beautiful, "the flowers were blossoming profusely and the grass was richly green," not unlike other days. The lottery would only take two hours and everyone would be home in time for lunch. Tessie even forgot what day it was, because it was like any other day. The children are playing and the townspeople are joking. This air of normality contributes to the horror.

3. The ritual occurs every June 27th when the townspeople gather on the green and the man of the family picks a slip of paper for each family member from a black box. Once the family is chosen, all members give back their slips and redraw. The person with a black dot is stoned. The terrible irony is that no one remembers "why" they stone one of their neighbors to death every year.

4. Old Man Warner represents the conservative, traditionalist view that what was good enough for the past is good enough for the future. He sees nothing but trouble in changing the old ways. Mr. Summers is thoroughly official from beginning to end. His job is to see that the lottery runs smoothly, not to consider its meaning. Nancy's friends, like Tessie, are passive until one of their own is threatened. They and Tessie probably represent the majority of the townspeople in their views.

5. The horror of the story is that Jackson's description of the event is not unbelievable. The town is a small, ordinary town with ordinary daily routines and inhabitants. The characters are as average as is the setting.

6. The townspeople do not want to challenge tradition, although they do not recall its origins. The point that Jackson is making is that the group can be dangerous for its unwillingness to examine its actions or the consequences of those actions. The town is a metaphor for our culture, which has ceased to question the reasons for its behavior.

Writing Topics (p. 616)

1. As a prewriting activity it may be important to define <u>scapegoat</u> and discuss how it relates to this essay. With the definition in mind, students can research other scapegoat rituals and the cultures that practiced the rituals.

2. After students have completed this assignment you can share the results with them in regard to the range of rituals identified in the essays. You may find a consistency in the kinds of rituals the students decided to discuss, or you may discover some unique and interesting cases. Whatever the result of your analysis, your discussion can give students a more comprehensive look at the role ritual plays in our family lives.